autism's
stepchild

autism's stepchild

a mother's story

Phyllis Grilikhes

REGENT PRESS
BERKELEY, CALIFORNIA

PAPERBACK
ISBN 13: 978-1-58790-373-1
ISBN 10:1-58790-373-3

E-Book
ISBN 13: 978-1-58790-374-8
ISBN 10: 1-58790-374-1

Library of Congress Control Number: 2016950448

Manufactured in the U.S.A.
REGENT PRESS
Berkeley, California
www.regentpress.net

Upon childhood arrangements
In the holy water of parents
bestowed on the child
Upon knowing that within the shell
the egg is not always pure

Table of Contents

Preface

I HAVE NEVER STOPPED THINKING and caring about Jean. As a psychology professor at a college in the San Francisco Bay Area, I told her story many times to students who were always deeply moved, had questions, and wanted to know more. Recently retired after almost three decades of teaching and mentoring students, I am ready to open the pages of the past and reveal the complete story of Jean, who in 1979 was the subject of my doctoral dissertation.[1] Dr. Mervin Freedman, dean of my graduate school, said, "You should publish this."

He felt that the case of this unusual girl ought not to be lost, because few persons with her disorder had been observed for such a long period of time. Also, born before autism was identified as a separate clinical entity, Jean suffered throughout childhood from the confusion of misdiagnosis.

Jean's mother, Dora, an intelligent, articulate woman, was vitally involved with her daughter's well-being. Upon hearing that I wanted to tell Jean's story in my thesis, Dora said, "That's good. Now I won't have to do it!" Dora and I decided we would embark on this project together. I would go to her house throughout the summer months of 1978 to tape-record her account of her daughter's life, while Jean would be occupied in a daytime activity.

My connection to Jean and her mother was established a long time ago. Now, with time available and Dora's emphatic words still clear in my memory, I am ready to tell the story.

This book is dedicated to Dora, in gratitude for entrusting me with the task.

PART I

A Chance Meeting

CHAPTER 1

Jean and Dora

ONE SUMMER EVENING in the mid 1950's, I was drawn to the sound of lively music in a park in Berkeley, California. I found a throng of people who, seeing the guitar on my shoulder, invited me to join them in folk singing and dancing.

The group consisted of parents and children from the Berkeley Activity Center for emotionally disturbed children. Responding to their invitation, I played my guitar and almost immediately my eyes caught and followed the excited, rhythmic rocking of a slender, dark-eyed girl. She appeared to be no more than twelve or thirteen. I was surprised to find out later that she was almost nineteen.

Her face was lit with a trance-like smile. She clapped her wrists together and her hands were twisted in what seemed like a frozen snarl. In obvious enjoyment of the music, her small and well-proportioned frame made contorted, rigid, repetitive movements. Her body seemed to be made of wire.

I was entranced by her movements and curious about her oddness. She would suddenly tilt her head to one side and press her thumbs behind her earlobes as though trying to blot out sound. Was one part of her enjoying the music, and another part trying to screen out other sounds?

Her mother stood close by and watched her with a warm concern. Introducing herself as Dora, we talked easily together. She explained that because there had been no school or group or center that would accept her daughter Jean, she had helped form the Berkeley Activity Center for Jean and others with similar problems.

Dora told me that Aron, her husband, and their young son, Mark, did not know how to interpret Jean's peculiar behavior. For example, her obvious fascination with the on-off buttons of light switches, and the way she smiled and hugged machines—such as a vacuum cleaner— whining loudly if anyone tried to interfere or stop her. For most people, language is a way of giving and receiving messages, but for Jean it often led to misunderstandings and frustrations. Machines and inanimate objects seemed easier to relate to than people.

Dora revealed that Jean had recently been released from Langley Porter Neuropsychiatric Institute in San Francisco after four years as an inpatient and was now being seen as an outpatient three times a week.[2] Dora and Aron had total care of her every day, without relief, except for the few hours she spent at the Center. Dora asked if I would be interested in coming to their home on a daily basis to "do music" with Jean. Eager to learn more about Jean I agreed.

Dora visited me at my house the next day, and the morning after that I began my work with Jean.

Our serendipitous meeting in the park led to a profound relationship with Jean and Dora that would be enmeshed in my life for years.

CURIOUS ABOUT WHAT I would find, I arrived the next day with my guitar. Jean, after a momentary glance, gave me the feeling that I had been dismissed. Even though she knew I was there, I felt an unaccountable space between us in the room.

Eager to find out about the unusual way in which she experienced the world, I would soon discover that Jean was acutely aware of everything that went on between us. Watching her whimsically cavort around the room that first day, I wondered, is she part elf?

Careful not to push, I offered a walk. She

agreed by coming to my side and facing the door. We walked about a mile from the quiet hill section of the city down to the flat everyday streets. After a while she allowed me to take her arm. We sang songs. She especially liked "You Are My Sunshine" and sang sweetly, perfectly in tune, sometimes clapping along to accentuate the rhythm. I liked to think that our voices blended well together.

On one of my visits, she ran to the corner of her room, tilted her head, and placed her hands behind her earlobes in great concentration. "What are you hearing?" I asked.

In an annoyed staccato voice she rasped, "Shhhhh ... 'Oh Susanna' backwards." Respectfully, I stepped back, amazed that she could do that.

Outdoors we often walked arm in arm and suddenly she would spring forward, crouch down to the ground, and touch the pavement with a light brush of her knuckles. Then she would backtrack and retrace her steps, tapping her foot lightly on a spot here and there. At times she would abruptly be caught up in a compulsive round of movements punctuated by quick cuppings of her hand to mouth, as though siphoning air through her fingers. She murmured what seemed like a brief catechism about germs in the air and needing to breathe them out. Her strange behavior in public did not make me uncomfortable, as it did—understandably—her mother, who worried that people would think Jean was poorly trained.

At the end of each day I shared with Dora what we had done and how Jean had behaved.

She expressed her desire that Jean would have a life beyond her immediate home and neighborhood, even beyond what I was providing for her, and wondered how to bring that about.

I often observed the interaction between mother and daughter as Dora tried to understand Jean's needs and wants. If Jean was not understood, she would pound the side of her head in what seemed to be utter frustration. I was glad to briefly take Jean off her hands.

Welcoming the opportunity to get to know her better, I would try to read a situation and ask myself, what is going on here between the two of us? I like to think that over the years I worked with her we had some good times together.

Jean's perceptual sensitivities to color and sound interested me. I was a young dancer at the time and also studying music. I identified with her quickness and ease of movement. We also resembled each other physically; both dark-haired, lithe, and slender. Although her oddness was a huge price to pay, she had a certain freedom to express herself without inhibition. She could turn a paint jar upside down, splash paint on walls, and not appear concerned with anyone's reaction. She managed to leap over and not be concerned with consequences.

Without her impediment, I had less freedom of expression. I was often bothered by the judgment of others, worried over the value of my performance or the consequences of failure. How could I come closer to what I observed to be Jean's freedom, without crossing the line?

Musing in particular on her keen sense of rhythm and color, I wondered if a similar state of mind existed in artists, people with a strong creative urge. Do artists become so inundated with an inspiration that they feel drawn to express several levels of feeling at the same time? Is there a connection between the enigma of Jean and artists' obsessiveness over their work? When Jean paints, she might stop at a certain point, leaving her work fragmented and repetitive, while at other times she worked toward completion as any artist works toward a goal.

Over many months my connection with her grew, and I observed that, for whatever reasons, her ability to communicate had been shortchanged.

Jumping around, whining in a high-pitched voice, hitting the side of her head, Jean seemed frustrated and lonely. Empathizing with what I perceived to be her loneliness, I reached out respectfully, tried to be responsive, and made an effort to understand. I found myself protective and gentle with her. My own fears rested, my self-doubt rested, I felt safe in a zone free of betrayal. I liked to think that she felt a receptiveness in me and that a special kind of friendship was growing between us.

Jean seemed to have an inability to recognize faces. Before letting me in the door, she required that I recite the names of my father and mother (which she had asked for when we first met). This ritual became a nuisance and my apparent annoyance with it caused the routine to lessen over time.

Her humor, oblique intelligence, and awareness astounded me. For example, she had memo-
rized all twelve street names that we had driven
through to get to the park, and on the way home
said, "Turn here, Grilikhes" when my mind had
been elsewhere.

During an outing one day at the neighborhood
swimming pool, I said, "Jean, I am going to do a
few laps. Please wait here for me." When I returned
she was asking the curious swimmers who'd gathered around, "Are you Phyllis?" Or I'd find her
masturbating in the pool. "Jean, not here," I'd say.
I think she stopped not because she realized it was
inappropriate, but because I asked her to. I felt
like a sister and protective of her in public.

Many times I was an unwilling witness to
her seething fury at her mother. Without apparent cause, Jean would burst forth with loud wail-
ing and whining that would accelerate and erupt
into pummeling the arms and clawing the hands
and whatever else she could reach of her mother.
Dora would stand still as she was being hit and
scratched, pleading with Jean to tell her what the
matter was. She seemed unable or unwilling to
use her strength to stay Jean's wild hands. Her
whining and hitting would grow more intense,
until finally, out of exhaustion and frustration,
she would stop, her body would collapse, and she
would sob remorsefully.

CHAPTER 2

My Time Away

I WORKED WITH JEAN almost daily for four years, and deep connections formed between the three of us. To think about leaving Dora and Jean was difficult. But the time had come. Since beginning my work with Jean, I had also been trying to build a dance and folk-singing career; I had been studying classical piano and caring for my infant son. All of these brought lots of joy, but meager income. Dora understood my need to move on.

One day as I was preparing to leave, Dora took me aside and with a quiet urgency said, "Please don't forget Jean." I assured her I would not. Yet at the same time I wondered where we would all be in the years ahead.

In the decades after I left, I sought opportunities where I could contribute to others and incorporate my interests and experience. I found jobs in community centers working with children and young adults in music, dance, and drama. I loved it.

Later, as a community service representative for a municipal agency, I helped people who were being forced to leave their homes due to neighborhood redevelopment. I became aware of the fear and anxiety inherent in a person's displacement from their familiar surroundings.

Eventually I enrolled in college to become a psychologist. While a graduate student in the 1970's, I worked as an activities therapist for a social service agency that offered a daily program for schizophrenic patients recently released from hospitals, who were on medication and living in board and care homes in the city.

Residents were bussed in from their homes and every Wednesday they tramped upstairs to play Bingo. After a month of calling numbers, I planned a strategy to stimulate their interest in other activities. In an adjacent room I set up a coffee machine, and the aroma floated into the hallway. A welcome sign at the door brought in a curious face and soon, a hand around a coffee cup. On one table there were planks of wood and sandpaper. Another table was strewn with bags of colored yarn and knitting needles. Curious individuals wandered over to the tables and after handling the supplies started working with them, perhaps recalling times when they had known how to build shelves or knit. These worn-looking individuals were functioning beyond the trap of their mental illness, and Bingo had been successfully challenged.

It was a pleasure to see a room full of former hospital patients come alive in this way.

Continuing to work as an activities therapist in board and care homes while preparing for my doctorate in psychology, I discovered Erik Erikson's now-classic book, *Childhood and Society*.[3] Reading the chapter "Early Ego Failure: Jean," I was astounded. Erikson described the special child, I had worked with many years earlier.

He wrote about Jean's winsome appeal and the way she used a negative statement to express a positive desire: "We're not going now" instead of, "Are we going now?" Erikson described her life before I met her, and noted Dora's puzzled and frustrated efforts to understand her daughter's atypical behavior. Jean's responses written about in his chapter did not surprise me; they were congruent with the Jean I had known. Reading the chapter, I was filled with the warmth of remembering, and knew that I had to find Dora and Jean again. It had been over twenty years.

I PHONED DORA and she invited me to visit. In Dora and Jean's familiar presence, I felt as if I'd never been gone. Jean didn't leave the room, pound her head, or turn away, but smiled and seemed glad to see me. Old friends, of which she had few, received a special welcome.

I was delighted to see the changes in her. Her hands were no longer gnarled. She sat in the room, concentratedly knitting while I spoke with Dora. It was the summer of 1978, I visited often and told Dora of my developing interest in writing Jean's story as my doctoral dissertation in psychology. We talked over the idea, she was thoughtful at first, then pleased and willing to help. Over the summer, she opened closets and drawers full of old material: books, pamphlets about childrearing, Jean's first pair of tiny shoes, an old birthday hat, a crayon drawing of a yellow flower.

We sat together often as Dora told me her story. She talked and read from her diaries while I captured her words on a tape recorder. Tired of the constant burden of daily caring and decision-making for her inscrutable child, she seemed to welcome the opportunity to examine the crises and solutions of Jean's difficult life over the past decades.

Dora's intelligent face lit with a bright smile and captivated me as I hunted the depth of her eyes for answers to my questions. Her story eventually became my graduate thesis: "Case Report: Follow-up Study of Erik Erikson's Jean."

Before continuing to write about Jean I had a strong urge to talk with Erikson. Would he be willing to share some of the impressions he had gathered long ago during Jean's very early childhood, before I knew her?

HE ANSWERED THE PHONE when I called. Introducing myself, I made clear the reason for my call, telling him that his chapter on Jean evoked memories of the years I had spent in close association with her during her late girlhood and young adulthood—after the period in which he had worked with her and her family. I told him I planned to do a follow-up study of her journey to the present day. He was interested and we set an appointment to meet.

Meeting him was unforgettable. A tall, stalwart man, casually dressed, with intense blue eyes and a shock of white hair opened the door and graciously welcomed me into his elegant home. It was uncluttered, with shining hardwood floors. Beautiful handwoven rugs collected from his travels hung on the walls. We sat facing each other in the living room, and his easy manner allowed me to relax enough to converse comfortably. He asked many questions. He wanted an update on Jean and said he regretted not remembering her birthday in the last few years.

His unassuming manner made it hard for me to believe I was talking casually with a world-famous figure. He shared memories of how confused Jean and her family had been when he first met them, and how after a while everyone grew more at ease as they took part in the curious undertaking of trying to understand and relate to the puzzle of Jean.

I left knowing I had been in the presence of wisdom, because for the entire afternoon he had not used one word of psychological jargon.

As I was leaving, he noted with heartfelt regret that his deep and concentrated attention on Jean and the enormity of her problems had caused him to neglect to pay attention to Mark, her brother.

My afternoon with Erik Erikson reinforced my desire to tell Jean's story.

PART II

Jean's Story Unfolds

This section of the book is based on my conversations with Dora as she looked back over two decades after our initial meeting. During our interviews, Jean was forty-five years old and out with a companion while we talked.

Though Jean was studied and written about by Erikson in the years before I met her, this part of the story has never been revealed to the public. In telling it, I am honoring a mother's request: "Please don't forget her."

NOTE: Dora referred to many organizations and resources that may no longer exist. Where I could not always find updated information for these references, I have used the names as she stated them.

CHAPTER 3

Beginnings and a Search for Answers

DORA WAS BORN IN 1902 and died in 1990 at the age of eighty-seven. Her ancestry in the United States extends back to before the American Revolution. Her forebears were hardy and tenacious, strong-willed and pragmatic, interested in community affairs and education. These same qualities sifted through the generations and unfolded again in Dora, whose mother was a staunch and belligerent champion of women's rights. Dora related how, as a small girl, she had marched beside her mother in a suffragette demonstration, carrying a banner. Her mother raised three girls, and Dora, as the youngest, barely remembered her father, who died when she was five.

She described her mother as loving but strict and controlling. She fostered Dora's interest in books but not her desire for dancing lessons.

Her mother sent all three girls to Vassar, then an exclusive women's college.

Dora grew into a radical, intellectual young woman interested in equality and justice, with a love for theater and the artistic milieu. When she was fourteen she had already glimpsed the exciting world outside of her mother's counsel. She had discovered and began to frequent a nearby bookstore, a gathering place of artists, writers, and musicians.

In the early 1920's, when she was eighteen, she met Aron, a gifted writer and the antithesis of her mother's choice. He didn't seem driven by the need to strictly obey society's rules, but followed his own inclinations.

Aron was small of stature, emotionally intense, with a sensitive, artistic nature. He was phobic in that he would gag at the mention of the words "dust" or "dirt" and at the touch of satin or velvet. He was often unpredictable, Dora said, but his clever, engaging sense of humor compensated for the irregularities in his personality.

According to Dora, he was delightful and they shared intellectual tastes in books, theater, and art. Dora and Aron eloped. "That was the first thing I'd ever done out of my mother's control, and she was furious." They lived in the Greenwich Village of the 1920's and wanted children. Mark was born in 1931, Jean in 1934.

Dora expressed that she was neurotically inadequate in matters of childcare and tended to feel overawed by medical professionals. As a result of this tendency she turned in strict adherence to the work of John Watson, a behavioral psychologist whose tenets of childcare included a denial of maternal instincts.[4] He advised mothers to resist their natural desire to kiss, cuddle, rock, or pick up a crying baby.

Dora claimed she agreed with Watson that a newborn is a tabula rasa—a blank slate—and that expression of motherly instincts would encourage a clinging dependency. "Jean's needs were attended to mechanically and on schedule according to the precepts of behaviorism, with a vengeance," Dora said. "I wasn't severe. I was rigid."

Despite her belief she was doing right, these restrictions were at times difficult for Dora. For instance, she desperately wanted to nurse her infant daughter, but nursing was frowned upon. In the wake of uncertainty, Watson's disapproval, and her own guilt, she nursed Jean for about one week. "It seemed all right for Jean," she said, but it wasn't all right for me. There was no support from anyone and I became ill with a breast infection and could no longer nurse. At the same time Jean got thrush, a mouth infection, which made it difficult for her to drink. She vomited and cried a lot."

The first few months were fraught with

anxiety for Dora as she struggled with the desire to express love for her infant and the constraints imposed by the childcare methods she had chosen in the name of correctness.

When Jean was eight months old, Dora contracted tuberculosis. Her doctor isolated her from her family within the house, thinking he was giving her a great treat by allowing her to remain at home. Mark, Jean's brother, was sent to stay overnight in a residential nursery school. Jean was placed in a room across from Dora's, separated by a bathroom, where she was cared for by a zealous nursemaid obsessed with cleanliness. Dora would hear the nursemaid say many times during the day, "Ach baby, you stink" in warning and admonishing tones.

Dora did not like this woman but felt helpless to change the situation because she was ill. Aron left the childrearing to Dora. He came in and out of the house, busy with his writing. He would pass by Jean in her crib, smile at her, and leave. Aron believed that children were not fully aware until they could walk and talk.

Jean was abandoned for hours at a time in her crib. She could see her mother but not touch her. An excellent photographer, Dora took photographs and made films of Jean from her doorway. Early films show Jean intently rocking from side to side. In one film Aron bends over to pick her up and she does not respond, but rocks in her crib as though for survival.

After thirteen months, Dora's quarantine was lifted and Jean was permitted to enter her mother's room. Immediately Dora noticed that something was wrong with her. "She screamed when I set her on the flowered rug. She recoiled from the pattern on the chair cover and seemed terrified of a furry ball that I rolled toward her. At the sound of the laundry paper crackling, she looked very anxious and cried fearfully. Her strange behavior was the beginning of problems."[5]

Jean tried to avoid being touched by anyone. She would not touch ashtrays or other dirty objects, and her fears increased.

She learned to walk and feed herself at the age-appropriate time but, according to Dora, by age two did not do much of anything else. Dora and Aron believed that except for her fearfulness, which they couldn't explain, she was probably a slow developer like Mark, who hadn't talked until he was four. In response to sounds, Jean would sometimes tilt her head to one side and press her fingers to her ears.

Other times she would stand in her crib, rock from side to side, and sing (without words) "Who's Afraid of the Big Bad Wolf," a popular song of the day. "She did not seem to reach out to anything or anybody, but became sad and silent."[2]

Facing Dora as I taped her story, I asked whether going back over those painful early days was hard for her. "Not really, "she said. "I am glad to finally talk about my feelings."

Dora continued:

When Jean was a year and a half, we traveled from California to New York to place her in the Bank Street Nursery School, known for its focus on all aspects of child development. Her teachers said she had an "emotional block." This meant nothing to us, and they didn't pursue it at all, still expecting that Jean was normal and would grow up to be like other children.

As she approached age three, the report from the nursery school stated that she made sounds and sang to herself but there were no words. She seemed to love the color of other children's paintings, was sensitive to surfaces, rubbing her hand very lightly over them. The teachers reported further that music was a strong interest, she came into the room as soon as she heard the sound of the piano. They also noted that she played individually, aloof from adults and children, and that she was aware of her surroundings even though it did not appear that she was.

When Jean was three, Dora and Aron placed her in the nursery school that Mark attended, in hopes that a new environment might stimulate more normal patterns of development. The director, Mrs. V, was a warm and gifted educator who was also tough, smart, and aggressive, bearing a resemblance to Dora's mother.

While Dora was away on a trip, Mrs. V sent her a report of Jean, who at that point was almost four. The report indicated a slight hopefulness, but also anxiety. It said Jean was even slower than Mark and that Mrs. V was really worried. Jean was past three and had no real use of language within normal limits for her age.

BECAUSE OF DORA'S BOUT with tuberculosis, she was not supposed to take full care of her children for about a year. "I took care of them Thursday and Sunday afternoons. It was very, very hard for me. I just got too tired."

At that time (the late 1930's and '40s), the only treatment for TB was rest. "After I had total rest for a little while, I was up for about one hour a day and that was increased up to twelve hours a day and that was once a week. The nap after lunch was a ritual and I had to have quiet. From the time Jean was two to six years old, that was the way things were."

According to Dora, Jean got along well with Mrs. V and was with her the whole time that Dora was unable to care for Jean, who at this stage was whining but not talking. Mrs. V reported that although Jean's speech had begun to gradually develop, she used meaningless echoing of words spoken by other people as well as their vocal intonations. "If Jean wanted a drink of water, she would say 'water,' 'tie my shoe,' or 'go for a walk,' not knowing which word or phrase would bring her the water. She did show a concrete understanding of what was said to her. If someone said, 'Did you lose your tongue?' she would quickly begin to look for it under pillows.[6]

At this point Mrs. V and Dora grew even more concerned about Jean's strange behavior. Dora wanted Jean to have a series of consultations with mental health professionals, but she lacked the confidence to handle this process herself. She decided that Mrs. V would act as her surrogate and take Jean to the East Coast to meet with professionals that Dora had identified. Dora was assertive, but simply did not trust herself with this task.

Mrs. V took Jean first to a psychologist, who suggested that Jean's parroting of speech (repeating what another person has said) indicated an emotional block meaning that for some reason the child had "turned against speech." Soon afterward, Jean began to use appropriate phrases as well as their vocal intonations. She would ask for a cracker by saying, "Do you want a cracker?" using a reversal of pronouns.

In New Haven, Connecticut, eminent child psychologist Arnold Gesell concluded that she was a slow-learning child and should be separated from her family.

A Massachusetts General Hospital psychiatrist was of the opinion that if a child is to have a severe mental disorder with a gross impairment of reality, Jean might be at the beginning of it.

Vassar psychologist Dr. Mary Fisher concurred and said, "If there is a psychosis of childhood, the only person in the world I can think of who might be willing to work with her is Erik Erikson. He has already written a paper about a girl whose description resembles that of Jean."

Adding to the confusion, Jean's pediatrician said, "I have known Jean since she was born, and she is perfect!"

One thing the consultants on Jean's journey agreed on, however, was that she should be taken away from her family.

Dora felt grossly uncomfortable at the idea of Jean living away from home, but was determined to do whatever the experts recommended. Mrs. V, acting in what she thought were Jean's best interests, took her, after a four-month absence from her family, directly back to the nursery school, where she would live at least temporarily. There Jean exhibited more psychotic behavior than before. She darted about, searched wildly for things, spoke in whispers, and developed rigid movements.

Jean became very attached to her blanket, a fetish Mrs. V decided was impeding Jean's development. Mrs. V therefore systematically proceeded to fractionate the blanket by degrees. She cut it in half, then in half again, until what remained was a small square that quickly became a frazzled rag the size of a handkerchief. Jean developed a new fetish around handkerchiefs, calling them "sheets." She began to sleep with her head under a pillow, clinging to a "sheet," which she made into a ball pressed against her mouth and held fast between her teeth. Was the "sheet" a symbol for her mother, who, while held, couldn't go away again? [7]

At Christmas Dora and Aron took Jean home from the nursery school for the weekend. The morning of her return to the school she carried in her arms all the presents she had received: jacks, dolls, a musical top and other toys. When her parents let her out of the car, she threw the presents in the gutter, stomped on them, and cried wildly. Dora recalled how painful it had been to watch. Jean was clearly a picture of despair as she was led back into the nursery school.

CHAPTER 4

Erik Erikson

I N THE EARLY 1940'S when Jean was six, Dora contacted Erik Erikson, as recommended by Vassar psychologist Mary Fisher, and took Jean to see him.

Not yet famous, he was gaining widespread attention in the psychoanalytic world for his innovative thinking, especially in his work with children. He was the first in his field to show an interest in Jean.

For one month, Erikson saw Jean several times a day. After a month of daily consultations, he arranged to visit her with her family every week. His visits continued, at least monthly for the next five years.

At the start he saw that both child and mother were suffering intensely from their separation.[8] Yet, contrary to professional opinion at the time, he did not blame Dora for Jean's problems. He felt he could not form a clear diagnosis of Jean until an attempt was made to readjust her to her family. Moreover, he felt that Dora was too dependent on Mrs. V.

He suggested an experimental period during which the family would live together again. Interviewing each family member separately, he explained Jean's development and the slow but definite progress she was making. He helped each person, including Mark, clarify their guilt or annoyance over the burden of having such a child in the house. His main objective was to try to bring Jean to the point where she could relate to people.

By restoring the mother/child relationship, with larger doses of mothering as a therapeutic remedy, he thought that Jean might establish avenues of expression with other family members as well. This might lessen her anxiety and make her a better subject for psychotherapy. Dora was willing to follow whatever Erikson suggested, and allowed herself to feel some hopefulness about the future.

Erikson saw that the family had many adjustments to make. At first Jean continued to relate emotionally only to machines. She would smile at them, whisper to them, and hug them. Then slowly she began to relate more to the family. However, upon greeting nine-year-old Mark with a radiant face and outstretched arms, she would suddenly grab his penis, which ensured his instant with-drawal from active cooperation in the experiment.

Jean warmed up to her father but attacked him in a similar way. Deeply interested in a lump on his hand, which she called "a lumpy," she loved him to smoke and blow smoke in her face. Yet at times she would rip the cigarette out of his mouth and throw it on the floor.

Erikson reasoned that these attacks were expressions of Jean's partial relationship to objects (including people). Her attacks were her way of testing the safety of relating to the whole object.

Jean spent hours sitting on her mother's lap, and slept with her as well, receiving the same kind of attention an infant would have received. She showed great improvement. Her movements became more graceful, and she began to play. Her vocabulary also grew.

On one occasion, while she was telling her little black dog to "go to sleep dog, stay under covers," she looked up at Dora with a rare direct glance and said, "Not go on long train ride some-time." Dora reassured her that the family would stay together.

Erikson noted that Jean was learning to link words to feelings. Given her relatively small vocab-ulary, they were now surprised to hear her say "nasty means naughty, means bad, means silly, means unpleasant" or "ashamed means mad, means cross, means annoyed."

He also observed that when she was seven, her fingers became representations of herself as well as her main means of aggression. She learned the letters of the alphabet by drawing them with her fingers. She learned to play melodies by scratching a xylophone with her nails. But she also attacked people by poking fingers in their eyes.

Among Jean's improvements during this period with Erikson was her musical ability. Dora explained:

> *Between the first of February, when Jean showed such interest in the xylophone, and just a few weeks later, I noticed that she would play it with her fingernails. This was typical of the way she learned something if it interested her. She would steal up on it and slide into it and suddenly prove to have learned it all by herself.*
>
> *She does it so one can hardly distinguish what she is doing. Tonight I discovered she could play "Water, Water, Wildflower" all the way through. This song requires every note in the scale. I asked her for it again and watched her hand travel up and down the scale as she thought where the next note was.*

I was amazed and made a big fuss over her, saying it was wonderful. I said, "Let's go downstairs to Mark and father and play it for them." Jean played it for Aron and Mark, who were astounded. She then played several other things. We all praised her and she ate it all up. She did not want to go upstairs, but seemed to want to stay and play on for the audience, a new delightful feeling for her.

Dora felt that what was happening was memorable and recorded the date in her diary: "Today, March 4, 1941, when Jean was seven, she got out the xylophone and played for one-half hour. I asked for several new songs, which I had heard her play, some quite hard like Brahms' 'Lullaby.' She can pick out any tune and perseveres until she succeeds."

At age nine, Jean began to pay keen attention to her mother's piano playing. One day she went to the piano and began to pick out melodies and harmonies that she'd heard her mother play. Jean played the entire first page of a Beethoven sonata. For days she worked at it and became quite frustrated when her small hand could not make the stretches needed to play a chord without rolling it (playing individual notes instead of playing them at the same time). She finally was able to play the first page just as she had heard it, without error. The family was stunned. Otherwise, her condition remained the same in that she still parroted speech—it simply was not an intrinsic part of her. She used neologisms (nonsense words), and in general her relationship to her social environment remained tenuous and peripheral.

In spite of Jean's progress and her musical ability, Dora's diary expressed her growing concern:

> *In some ways I have been more discouraged and anxious about Jean than at any other time in two years. The withdrawn behavior, the waving of hands, laughing at unseen things have not disappeared; instead they seem to have increased. She whines or plays alone with water or sand or carries on her own play in her own peculiar way too much of the time.*
>
> *My anxiety during these weeks about Jean is increasing. Compulsive neurotic queer behavior and our inability to snap her out of it, leads to many conversations, some with Aron, some with Mark. We have to discuss with Erikson our whole approach to this kind of behavior. Up to now we have thrown ourselves into her fantasy play.*

*We always cooperate, and try to lead
it on in order to let her get something out of
her system, to try and understand better
what is bothering her. I feel that in the last
two weeks there has been so much of it,
that we sink into kind of a bewildered and
defeated frame of mind and we feel helpless in relation to it. In my case this leads
to great anxiety, and I can see the others,
Aron and Mark, becoming depressed.*

Dora explained further that after many fail-
ures to interest Jean in various activities, she
finally achieved some success one day when she
was weeding the garden. Jean began to work
alongside her and the next day asked to do some
weeding again. The satisfaction Jean gained from
weeding gave Dora the notion that she had been
neglecting the work side of things (tasks such as
gardening and cleaning) as a way of helping Jean
out of her moods.

It seems possible that when Jean found certain activities or tasks satisfying for whatever reason, like weeding in the garden, or musical engage-
ment, she was able to give her focused attention
while involved, and detour past her mental illness.
(I was reminded at that moment of how years ago,
the knitting and shelf-building tasks I had offered
to a group of mentally ill individuals had helped

them, while engaged, to bypass their illness.)

Erikson continued to help Jean work through much of her need for dependence on Dora, but there were still puzzling behaviors to cope with in that she was deeply concentrated one moment and without endurance the next.

He felt that the concepts Jean had formed were not lost, but simply overshadowed by her next crisis. He believed it might be possible at that point for her to make a transference (a close emotional tie) from her mother to a psychiatrist who could further guide her intellectual and social learning.

In a diary passage written when Jean was ten, Dora expressed deep frustration over the burden of Jean's total dependence on her to offer satisfying activity, all day, every day:

> *All in all, Jean has matured so much in the last six months. In the deeper emotional relationship with us, and in having acquired many new skills. It is not surprising that we have a whole new set of problems to face. I think we have to face first of all that I am no longer the complete satisfaction to Jean that I was.*
>
> *She needs more people in her world; there isn't enough variety or experience in our backyard. In many ways, she is*

an eleven-year-old, confined and bored and extremely irritable. She is also willfully destructive, which she never used to be, a sign of frustration. She often yells now instead of the old whining out of pure meanness. We have reached a sort of impasse and we are getting on each other's nerves.

The next most outstanding fact about Jean at present is that in these very difficult days, the only happy moments are the study hours. So eager is she for reading and arithmetic that I have been able to move them to the morning from the bedtime period. She sits down willingly to work, works hard for an hour, and when I am ready to quit, she will say, "Do arithmetics."

I write a page of forty problems in addition, to which she has to write the answers, and she goes to it with a will. She is hungry for some kind of grind and to this she is willing to accept a schedule.

I don't allow piano playing any time of night anymore, or reading, or stories. I know that her drive won't be curbed by a conventional bedtime.

Her naughtiness, her screaming, her lingering sex behavior problem, her *destructiveness, to my mind are more normal behaviors than at any time in the past. Only they have to be met in a more normal way than we are meeting them. It isn't normal to be a sort of prisoner at age eleven—or five or six, if that is closer to her level of development. It is normal to meet such problems in a school group.*

Because there was no daily plan for Jean and she was not able to make her needs known, Jean's aggressiveness toward Dora continued, sometimes in an extreme manner, as the following excerpt from my conversation with her indicates:

Dora: She was hanging on a bar in the playground, swinging and enjoying it. Suddenly she kicked me very hard in my chest. I thought, she knows better than that.

PG: Did you say anything to her?

Dora: I probably didn't say anything and I thought, She's crazy. But that was nothing to what came later.

PG: You didn't tell her that it hurt?

Dora: She wasn't even angry at me when she kicked me. I didn't tell her that it hurt. I didn't tell her anything like that.

PG: It must have been an awful moment

*for you when you saw that she seemed
to have no feeling and you felt that she
was crazy.*

*Dora: I didn't express my true feelings to
her because I didn't think Jean understood. I couldn't get to her. I was relating
to her in nursery-school fashion, speaking
to her slowly and clearly, not expecting
her to understand. I think this happened
at the time we decided, and Erikson
helped us decide, that she would have to
go into a home. It was too much for us.
It was too much for Mark, it was obvious
now that he never invited anybody home,
and he was suffering from this. I was
depressed all the time. I was very angry
that she didn't have any school, that we
couldn't get any babysitting. I couldn't get
any relief. I was locked into the situation.*

Dora recalled how the family was terrified
from the time Jean was two that they might do
something wrong. The childrearing books Dora
read made her feel terribly insecure and afraid
that if they did something wrong, the trauma
would ruin their child's life.

In contrast, Erikson's attitude was that if
Dora made a mistake, she'd correct it. "He backed
us up, he had confidence, was appreciative, and

made me feel good about everything that I did."

While working with Jean, Erikson had made progress in that she had begun to use speech. Even though the speech had been well articulated, it was not initially used for communication. It was said as though to herself. She did eventually communicate in her own way through the use of metaphor, neologisms, or echolalia (parroting speech). It became clear to her parents that she had capabilities that for some unknown reason she was unable to express. None of these hoped-for improvements emerged, however, and her growth and development remained abnormal.

CHAPTER 5

Attempts at Treatment

I N DECEMBER 1945, Erikson arranged for Jean to be seen at the Menninger Clinic in Topeka, Kansas for possible admission to the Southard School, which was under the jurisdiction of the Clinic.[9] Jean was to stay at the Clinic for two weeks while being tested. If the test results were favorable, she would enter the Southard School.

In January 1946, Aron and Dora received a letter from the clinic stating that Jean had an emotional illness. She was "too disturbed" to be accepted at the school, but the doctors offered two treatment possibilities: either continue with the present method of care at home, or enroll her in a psychiatric school prepared to cope with her problems. They diagnosed Jean's condition as childhood schizophrenia.

The letter contained a summary from the

psychologists' report, which described suc-
cinctly the symptoms later known to be Kanner's
Syndrome, without diagnosing it as such. The following is an excerpt from the summary:

> *Jean's speech shows bizarre fea-
> tures. She talks in alternately high pitched
> and low pitched tones, enunciation was
> clear but her speech is often unintelligible
> because of its fragmentary character and
> the frequent use of neologisms.*
>
> *Sometimes she tries hard to be under-
> stood and the more urgent her desire, the
> more incoherent her speech becomes. At
> times she speaks intelligibly and clearly,
> either in answer to a question or in the
> context of play activities.*
>
> *She was observed reprimanding
> herself for pulling at her sweater using a
> different voice from her usual one saying,
> "You pulled your sweater, you will spoil
> it." Her movements were awkward and
> peculiarly rigid.*
>
> *At times she clapped her hands and
> grimaced, at other times she threw her-
> self on the floor and kicked. When she
> became angry, she bit her hand saying,
> "Bit myself off—make it bleed—I will die."*

After Jean's stay at the Menninger Clinic, with its many preparations and the possibility of acceptance, only to be followed by rejection, she developed a new habit. If she brushed by a certain chair or stepped on a threshold, she would go back and retrace her steps, go out and come in, over and over. This behavior appeared after she had returned home.

Did this compulsive repetition relate in some way to her repeated anticipations and rejections? Is it possible that these behaviors were not random but, as in pantomime, a way of speaking? If Jean had been able to express her feelings in language, she might have said, "I am feeling confused. Help me."

Dora and Aron were understandably discouraged by the rejection. This was the first time Jean had been diagnosed with an extreme condition, and the clinic's suggestion that she be sent to a psychiatric school disturbed them.

Despite the diagnosis, Dora and Aron continued to deny the seriousness of Jean's condition. She was bright and beautiful and they refused to believe all they had heard and read in the clinic's report. They were simply not ready to give her up. They kept Jean at home for another year, but the situation worsened to the point of becoming intolerable.

Dora had heard about the Bruno Bettelheim

Orthogenic School in Chicago, but Erikson recommended against it.[10] According to him, the school's educators incorrectly assumed that parents were always at fault, whereas Erikson believed causes were multiple and complex. He wanted Jean to remain with her family.

Erikson questioned the role of "maternal rejection" in Jean's case and talked of the possibility of a deficiency in the ability to interact with humans, which he called the "sending power" of the child toward the parent in early infancy.

In spite of the pressure Dora felt from Erikson to keep Jean at home, by the end of that year she didn't see an alternative. She and Aron were ready to consider the advice of the Menninger Clinic and send her away for good, preferably to a psychiatric school if one could be found. Erikson recommended the Emma Pendleton Bradley Home in Providence, Rhode Island.[11]

After all the trials and considerations, the family had made up their minds that they probably would never see Jean again. Erikson was aware that this could be the case.

Jean went to the Bradley Home in early 1946. After ten months she was discharged. This is a summary of the explanation sent to her parents:

*Jean had begun to be very destructive
of hospital furnishings and equipment,*

and of other children's belongings. In so doing she was interfering with group projects and routines which were part of the treatment for other children. The staff felt she showed a lack of progress and recommended training and treatment for her on a more individual basis. They felt that the school was not helping her and diagnosed her condition as childhood schizophrenia, stating that the outlook was entirely discouraging.

For Dora and Aron, Jean's discharge, after they had suffered the adjustment of deciding to send her away for good, was emotionally very hard to bear.

According to Dora, the authorities—namely Erikson and the doctors from the Bradley Home—decided that Jean should not be picked up from the school. They believed this would only reactivate the confused and painful emotional climate between Dora and Jean around reuniting and separating. Instead, Erikson arranged for Jean to be taken directly from the school to a newly opened children's ward at Langley Porter Neuropsychiatric Institute in San Francisco, where she would stay for six weeks for study and testing. One reason Erikson recommended Langley Porter was its new director of children's services, Stanislaus Szurek, who brought a psychoanalytic orientation to child psychiatry.[12]

Dora recalled the date as late February 1946, just prior to Jean's twelfth birthday. It was the last she would see of Jean for six months.

CHAPTER 6

Langley Porter

OF THE EIGHTEEN CHILDREN on the psychiatric unit, Jean was the only one who was clearly psychotic. Psychotherapy was attempted with some children who were being treated as outpatients, and parental participation was found to be of great value in this process. Stanislaus Szurek believed in collaboration—that is, parents as well as the child should receive individual psychotherapy. Clueing in to a parent's emotional balance often provided partial insight into the child's condition.

Although skeptical, Dora agreed for Jean's sake to participate in therapy. She had been through a long period of doubt and nagging anxiety that Jean was not normal. Consumed with guilt over the seriousness of Jean's condition, she was angry with herself. Having swung back and forth between hope and despair for so long, she was open to change but wondered how, and if, it was possible.

Aron, on the other hand, was reticent and resisted participation. He claimed that sessions would be difficult to arrange—the family lived in another city, he didn't drive, and transportation would be a problem. He also admitted it was difficult to visit Jean in the hospital because he could not bring himself to tell her why she couldn't live at home. Intuitively he sensed she was aware of his feelings and understood she was too sick and too much of an emotional drain on the family to live with them. It was hard for him to be frank, or express warmth or affection, with any member of the family, including Jean.

Jean's psychological tests on admission to Langley Porter indicated she had superior intelligence that could not be adequately tested because of severe emotional disturbance interfering with full performance and normal ways of thinking.

Therapy for Dora was suspended during Jean's initial hospitalization. After six months she received a letter from Erikson saying that Jean was doing everything possible to justify the diagnosis of childhood schizophrenia and that she was the most difficult child they had ever seen on the ward.

For example, she wouldn't get off the bed unless she had first put on her shoes, and when she was off the bed, her shoes were soon taken away to make her calm down. She'd defecate on the floor and urinate on the bed, things she'd never done in the past. However, Dora thought this behavior was understandable after all Jean had been through. In August of 1946 Jean wrote Dora a letter in which she said, "Come see me."

Dora described seeing Jean for the first time in six months: "She was smiling and looked taller. I didn't know what to expect. It was terrible, I mean I didn't want to see her really. Well, I don't know what I wanted. It was too confusing and too terrible. She smiled at us, looked away, and was dancing around and backtracking. We had never seen that gait before."

Both parents traveled from Los Angeles to visit her periodically for about a year. Once, after a two-day visit on a weekend, Jean said, "Go home on Sunday?" Dora said, "No dear." Jean said, "Go home on two Sundays?" Dora did not know at the time that Jean meant, "How many weeks am I going to stay here?"

Dora finally admitted to Jean that she did not know when she would be coming home. Szurek had told Aron and Dora throughout the therapy, "Be honest with her." He was pleased with this particular exchange between Dora and Jean; to him it was a turning point. In keeping with Szurek's philosophy, the nurses, too, were honest with the children on the ward.

"It was so welcome," Dora said. "The medical team seemed to imply that Aron and I were the ones who could help her. Before Langley Porter, everyone was continually separating us from Jean. Szurek repeatedly told us, 'You are the people who can help her'."

Szurek told his staff that if Jean was too difficult to handle, he would find some other place for her, meaning the state hospital, and that Langley Porter was her last chance. He left it to the staff to see what they could do, challenging them to do their best. This was his typical strategy.

Dora had mixed feelings about her private therapy sessions. At first she felt that the analysis was "designed to make you feel that there were all sorts of crazy, terrible things going on, that probably I was schizophrenic myself." But Szurek believed schizophrenia was not such a terrible thing, that it was one end of a continuum that began with a neurosis, and that it was all a question of degree. "Looking at it from that point of view," she said, "we are all schizophrenic."

Dora was encouraged to consider how she was affecting Jean's behavior and to ask herself: How am I involved in it? Am I getting some satisfaction from it? "Szurek believed that I was getting some reward from Jean's strange behavior and that I should understand it and take responsibility for my part in the manifestations of her behavior."

Jean stayed at Langley Porter for four years. Szurek's staff was devoted to helping her and kept careful notes of their observations and trials.

While interviewing Dora, I obtained permission from the Langley Porter medical team to use, for the purpose of telling her story, the case notes of the two nurses who had worked closely with Jean during her hospitalizations.

Nurse P tells the following in notes between 1946 and 1950:

> *On the ward Jean would attach herself to one person. She was content to walk with this person alone, becoming very resentful if another child interfered and would say "go away!" She was in a classroom for a short time each day and continued reading and basic arithmetic. When frustrated, this very small for her age, young teenage girl, wiry and strong, would fly into a rage, kick, pound, scratch, bite, or butt her head against a wall or bed or glass window. She would attempt to butt children, nurses, rip their clothing, and she broke windows with her feet.*
>
> *Her movements were quick. She darted skillfully. The staff used firm handling and mild restraint when she was in*

a rage. Afterwards she would sob, deep, racking sobs, looking sad and worn out. The staff gave her affection and tried to understand.

The following is a letter she wrote to her mother on her own initiative when she was thirteen: "Dear Mother and Father we love you very much mother and father are at home. Jean is a good girl. You are playing well Some day you will do what I ask you to do We didn't tell our mother to get to the park You sing a beautiful song very much Mother is very proud of you because you were singing very well. Some days what shall we do we play some songs alright we play some songs—after we play some songs should you read a book Should you play with toy? Would you like to not see your mother. would you rather do something we."

After a visit with her mother, Jean interrupted her drawing and said, "Don't drag your feet—you dropped it on the floor—you are so slow." *These phrases seemed irrelevant at the time, but it was later discovered that this kind of speech has special meaning for autistic children in that it is considered a delayed response to an emotional experience. She was repeating what had been said to her. When asked who said these things, she replied: "my mother."*

The occupational therapist reported that "Jean could operate the loom alone, but kept asking which pedal to press next. I told her to press the next pedal and not bother talking about it so much, at which point she ran across the room and kicked another therapist."

Nurse P. continued:

Jean perceived her body as a fearsome piece of machinery that she had to control lest it burst or get sick. She wouldn't eat her food for a long time because she thought it would break open her stomach.

When she resumed eating she would spit the food out and have no bowel movement and when the bowel movements came they were horrendous and hard. When you have to control everything and you haven't got the equipment to do it, it must be terrifying. Jean had to control everything or fight it. She couldn't trust, she couldn't accept.

She wanted people to let her be as she was, to follow her. She responded negatively to those who had an investment in teaching her, or to those who had hidden expectations or pushed for her to "get better." She craved a total human and intimate relationship, which is how I tried to relate to her.

Her mother was always trying to manage her, all external things like education and arts and crafts. What disturbed me when I heard her talk was that her attitude seemed more clinical than motherly.

There was a lot of concern and caring but she did not seem able to relax with her or be spontaneous. She'd much rather discuss Jean than to be with her—to sit and play with her. I think she believed that if you could somehow pull all the resources from everywhere and hand them to her she would blossom.

Jean parroted and talked in a stilted way. The ward was active and it was probably one of the best periods she ever had. She knew that the people in charge were predictable. There was always a lot going on and she was very much part of the ward activities.

WHILE JEAN WAS AT LANGLEY PORTER, Dora discovered an article about severe disorders of childhood, written in 1943 by Leo Kanner, a scientist at Johns Hopkins Medical School.[13] He identified a syndrome or set of symptoms important enough to separate from the mass of other childhood abnormalities and psychoses of childhood.

After summarizing the case histories of eleven children and pointing to the individual differences between them, his now-famous article clarified the differences.

According to Kanner, the set of symptoms were based on the following characteristics: extreme autistic aloneness, acting as if other people were not present, resistance to interference, a desire to be left alone, fascination with non-human objects, a strikingly intelligent appearance, insistence on sameness in the environment, excellent rote memory for names and places, precise recollection of complex sequences and patterns, essentially normal physically, and language disturbance—either mutism or language that does not seem intended for interpersonal communication.

Kanner labeled this syndrome "early infantile autism."

One of the major differences between early infantile autism and childhood schizophrenia as described by Kanner is that the autistic child shows extreme aloneness from the beginning of life, whereas the schizophrenic child withdraws into a world of unreality.

Kanner pointed out that another common denominator of early infantile autistic children is that their parents are often highly intelligent. He noticed that there could be a lot of parental obsessiveness. In fact, many of the parents, as did Dora, took copious notes and kept detailed reports over the years. Kanner also mentioned that in his original group there were "few really warm-hearted fathers and mothers."

He noted, too, that parents as well as grand-parents of these children tended to be preoccu-pied with scientific or literary abstractions and had a "limited genuine interest" in people. In spite of his observations, he stated pointedly that he did not attribute the entire disturbance of the child exclusively to early parental relations. He said, "It is possible that these children are born without the innate ability to form usual affective contact." He labeled this an "inborn autistic dis-turbance of affective contact."

Upon reading Kanner's article, Dora knew immediately that he was describing her child. Her initial reaction was anger and denial.

According to Kanner's concept, therapy such as the type Erikson was providing, as well as the psychotherapy Dora had undergone with Szurek, would be useless, and Jean's condition would therefore remain unmodifiable. Dora preferred at that time to live with the guilt of knowing about Kanner's article rather than deal with the possibility that Jean's condition was irreversible.

Dora didn't discuss the article with anyone. It was not in her nature to give up on a cause, and she was determined to continue exploring every possibility. She would do whatever was necessary in her own life to make restitution to Jean if that would alter her condition. Jean was her cause and Dora held on tenaciously.

As I listened to Dora's stark refusal to accept what she inwardly knew to be true about Jean's condition, I was struck by how powerfully important it was for her at that time to believe as she did.

There was no known treatment at the time for Kanner's Syndrome. So it was easy to see how Dora and Aron, not wanting to think of their daughter as permanently abnormal, would continue to impose normal controls on her behavior, yet become increasingly anxious and confused.

It took a decade before professional interest in Kanner's Syndrome began to appear in articles in psychological journals in the U.S. and abroad. Kanner intensified his studies and continued to publish, further clarifying his original material and giving credibility to his theories.

CHAPTER 7

Jean Returns Home

IN 1950, JEAN'S FAMILY, encouraged by the therapeutic team at Langley Porter, moved from Los Angeles to the San Francisco Bay Area. At that point Jean, discharged from inpatient services after four years, went to live at home and became an outpatient along with her parents.

Dora said that the most important gains from Jean's inpatient experience at Langley Porter were in the area of socialization. Therefore, the family expected something different from the last time she lived with them.

Jean's return, however, was hardly ideal. Mark had spent years in the army and completely lost tolerance for his sister's unusual behavior. Aron had experienced irreversible setbacks at work and now suffered from unabated depression, a stomach ulcer, and severe arthritis. He slept poorly at night and needed the house kept quiet during the day. Perhaps part of his condition was due to accumulated disappointment and a sense of utter failure with Jean. Was he slowly realizing that she would never be normal and that her care would be his and Dora's responsibility always? He also developed osteoporosis and as a result suffered great physical pain when Jean, in a burst of rage, would kick him. He felt as if they were living in a one-patient sanitarium.

At night Jean would get out of bed, making a ruckus in her own room and disturbing her mother's sleep in the next room. Dora said, "It was like having waking nightmares—she seemed to breathe fire. Jean would reach down to the floor, touching it many times, seeming aware of nothing but her rage."

Dora occasionally gave her sleeping pills, against the advice of the Langley Porter therapeutic team, who believed that hard times should be worked through rather than artificially subdued. "But they don't have to live with her," Dora said. The team ultimately encouraged Dora to do what felt comfortable, and she was grateful for this flexibility in their support.

Jean was in her early teens by then, and Dora inquired at the local school district about the possibility of education for her. A social worker arranged for a home teacher, who visited three times a week. At first Jean seemed excited and eager to learn, and tried hard. But then she lost interest and became physically abusive toward the teacher.

By this time both parents were desperate. They realized Jean needed some kind of daily program. But the discrepancy between her chronological age and her behavior was so marked it was hard to envision any school or group situation that would suit her.

During this frustrating period Jean once again began to violently attack her mother, who would drag her fighting from the street or car. Visits at one neighbor's house were scenes of kicking, scratching, and biting, torn clothing and bleeding wounds inflicted on Dora and the neighbor.

Sleeping pills for Jean wore off after an hour and a half. After Dora and Aron went to bed, they were likely to be awakened by the sound of furniture being broken and windows smashed.

Assaultive behavior occurred in public, at the Langley Porter clinic, and in and out of the car, to the point where Dora was afraid to drive alone with Jean. She was covered with bruises, scratches, and bites. She said that her therapist was "very stern" about these incidents, "He presumed that all the brawls were my fault." Yet in spite of the problems, Dora and Aron did not want to institutionalize their daughter.

AFTER JEAN HAD BEEN living at home for two years, Dora was desperate. She decided to develop a new kind of educational program that would serve the needs of Jean and other radically disturbed children. Neighbors who were business and education professionals, as well as friends and artists acquainted with the family, helped Dora organize and plan the program. After months of contacting parents of emotionally disturbed children in the public schools, an interested group of parents responded. They met and planned the opening of what was called the Berkeley Activity Center.[14]

Dora pushed for parental participation in operating the center, unlike—she recalled with chagrin—her experience at Langley Porter, where her participation in ward meetings and professional consultations about her child was firmly forbidden.

The philosophy of the center was that in addition to outpatient individual psychotherapy, which Jean and many other children were already receiving, the center would provide a social environment for them.

The center would also provide a much-needed respite for parents. The first program began in the summer of 1952 and was conducted in one room of a local school. Fourteen severely disturbed children attended. Although Jean was in her late teens, her small size and immature behavior made it possible for her to take part.

The Berkeley Activity Center was incorporated in the spring of 1953 as a nonprofit organization with six board members including Dora.

Jean went daily into a milieu of caring, sensitive people who worked at the center, where she painted, made music, and was less physically isolated. Assaultive behavior toward her mother subsided somewhat.

Dora's therapist at Langley Porter believed that her activities on behalf of building the center were an avoidance of her tasks with Jean. Dora said it was constantly held out to her that if the family would solve their own problems, Jean would get well. She described Szurek's attitude as "we at the hospital can't promise anything—there's a lot we don't know." But Dora felt that they knew more than she did, so she and Aron continued to participate in psychotherapy.

Although Jean often balked at going to the center, she seemed to enjoy herself once she arrived. She and Frankie Lemon, an artist who taught at the center, often painted together. Jean would copy an image Frankie had painted, but choose her own colors and details. Dora believed that Jean's experiences were recounted in the colors and figures she painted. Dancing and rhythmic activities such as playing simple instruments or singing songs were also of great interest to her. Dora described these activities as "delightful experiences among all the terrible ones at home."

The center's director, Lillian Weitzman, began to take Jean and two other children on special outings. They played tennis or made sandals and other craft items. Although Jean seemed to relax around some of the staff members, times at home were still tense and violent.

It was during this period, while Dora and Jean were part of the Berkeley Activity Center, that I first met them at the summer picnic described in the beginning of this book—and became Jean's first friend.

Ironically, after a year, the board of the center that Dora had helped to organize and establish voted to admit children only up to the age of twelve and Jean was twenty. Dora, who was no longer a board member at that point, argued against their decision, but the vote was unanimous. The center was now unavailable to Jean, and Dora, who remained as a committee member, felt the decision was unfair. During this period, I was working with Jean daily and witnessed Dora's bitterness about the vote.

Believing that Jean should be exposed to knowledge, Dora was determined to teach Jean herself. She shared her feelings with me:

How do I dare, all alone, to tackle these things which I know so little about? To Jean I am an authority on everything, no matter if I say, "I can be wrong" or "I don't know." Today Jean said to me, "I study, I am a studies." Triumphantly, I corrected her, "I am a student." She repeated, "I am a student." It was my turn to be hesitant and troubled. Wouldn't Jean sound ridiculous if she repeated this to others? So what, we are both students, truly.

Dora was at a turning point. How could she continue to be responsible for Jean's education and at the same time tend to a growing need for her own independence?

BY 1955, DORA HAD BEEN in therapy at Langley Porter for five years, and was noticing subtle changes in her attitude toward herself. She decided after some hesitation to attend her first college reunion (the thirty-first).

She was surprised and pleased to discover that most of her Vassar classmates shared her interest in ideas and books. "It was a fantastic experience with my roots, after which I decided I must work at something. Parents who had jobs and worked—survived."

Dora acted immediately on her decision by attending a job clinic while she was in New York for the reunion. "Everything seemed hopeless because I was fifty-three, and youth and veterans were preferred." But she also realized she had an edge over most of the other job seekers—a "gut confidence" she had not felt in the past.

The trip to New York allowed her to realize her new strengths, and on returning to California, she soon found a job as a market research interviewer.

Dora credited her many hours of therapy with having given her lots of interviewing experience. She found out that she could ask questions in a subtle manner and establish great rapport with interviewees. She went from this job to a cost analysis job and then to a research job investigating older women's problems in seeking employment. Her newfound confidence, she said, was a tremendous byproduct of therapy that she could not have anticipated.

This confidence led her to apply and get accepted to library school, even though she was twenty years older than the allowable entrance age. She obtained a library science degree in 1957, again giving credit to her therapy as having enhanced her feelings of capability.

In dealing with fellow library workers, she recalled: "I kept them informed about what was to be done. If they didn't do something they were supposed to do, I did it. I learned to manipulate people through guilt." To Dora's surprise, Szurek at Langley Porter was not opposed to her going to library school and working. She continued in therapy throughout her schooling and during her employment afterward.

In 1957, Aron's ill health and Jean's need for constant close supervision made it impossible to continue keeping Jean at home. Out of desperation, Dora and Aron decided to send her to Napa State Hospital in Northern California.[15] Jean's therapist at Langley Porter, aware of her impending state hospitalization, notified Dora of an immediate ten-day vacancy on the children's ward at Langley Porter, which would at least postpone Jean's move for a few days.

CHAPTER 8

Return to Langley Porter

JEAN RE-ENTERED LANGLEY PORTER and stayed for seven years. Soon after this admission she had a convulsive seizure, which prompted a neurological examination. She'd had two seizures previously, in 1953 and 1954 (at home).

The neurological report described her as having epileptic susceptibility, and stated that the seizures could have been caused by her parents' "sudden withdrawal of sedatives. Abnormality in the left occipital area was confirmed. On one occasion a paroxysm of high potential muscle activity appeared on the right side suggesting that some of the patient's behavior might reflect abnormal cerebral discharge."

During Jean's stay at Langley Porter, her parents were, as before, expected to participate in weekly therapy sessions. Aron's original reticence about therapy continued. Dora, however, came to therapy expressing pride and pleasure at having procured library training and a job. She recognized that therapy had not only increased her confidence but also helped her acknowledge and express her feelings more openly toward Jean and Aron.

Always eager for Jean to receive schooling, Dora persuaded Langley Porter to provide Jean with a private tutor for half an hour each day. She felt this was a big concession and wished they would offer even more.

Nurse M, who had worked with Jean during her first hospitalization, gives the following account of Jean's behavior over this second period:

> When I was directly in charge of Jean I had a chance to observe a wide spectrum of her behavior as well as the interaction between mother and daughter. I was assigned to Jean the first week I was there. Her mother was delighted to have me there.
>
> There was a lot of smiling, but there were a lot of comments about, oh you people come and go, get married and then you leave, you're going to let me down.
>
> It took a year of a whole lot of testing by Jean, and it was rough. There was

a lot of scratching and a lot of physical attacking.

I had to learn a lot about how to work in this kind of situation, how to get past my own feelings of anger. Eventually I went into therapy because I was so angry all of the time. A lot of nurses had to go into therapy in order not to react to all of that anger with more anger. You can't use rage back—it's a dead end.

I was just angry but my anger hadn't surfaced much before that. There were other abusive children there but Jean was the oldest. I remember one very dramatic time that helped me to understand more about the relationship between Jean and Dora.

We were going to the park, and Dora was going to take us. Jean was getting very compulsive about so many things. She seemed to anticipate them and get upset and worried. For instance, she would say, "Is it time to go, is it time to go?" to the point that the people answering her would get agitated and they would answer her and answer her and then she would say, "It's not time to go, is it time to go?"

I learned not to tell her anything until

I knew that surely something was going to happen. Just anticipating the picnic, she'd get worried because it "might rain." She seemed to feel that you could never trust life, people or any type of thing. She would say, "Is my mother coming?" "Is it not going to be your day off?" I was the charge nurse in addition to having full responsibility for Jean. I had to attend a lot of meetings, which irritated her.

One day we were going somewhere and she was in such a state about everything, that she couldn't possibly enjoy it even if it did happen. She would just sort of make a mess, pounding the side of her head, whining, kicking anything or anybody close by.

Jean's mother came one morning, and she always had this calmness and smile that made me very uncomfortable because it just didn't fit the situation. We went to a donut shop. Jean wanted some donuts and said, "I want a chocolate donut." Her mother said, "What about some nice sugar donuts?" Jean said, "I want some chocolate donuts"—very clearly stated.

She would not comply with the request for donuts, and bought sugar donuts, which made Jean crazier. However, they got in the car and Jean said, "Move the car back two inches," so her mother moved it back—back and forth, back and forth. "Open the door and get out." Her mother went through all of this compulsiveness with her. She would go along with some really bizarre request but she wouldn't go along with a straight request.

In another incident:

Jean said she wanted to go somewhere at 2 o'clock: "Will you come at 2 o'clock?" Her mother would smile benignly and say, "Yes we'll be there at 3 o'clock." An assistant nurse who worked with me at times always thought that Jean went bizarre after that; she would do all of this controlling stuff like touch, touch, touch. "She would get more and more compulsive around these little confrontations with her mother."

And an example of Jean's independence when not interacting with her mother:

She took a hard-boiled egg and jammed it into her mouth, and then put salt and pepper in her mouth. I said,

"Ugh, Jean that's not the way to eat an egg, "and she said, "Is it your egg?" which I thought was gorgeous.

Jean made major strides forward from 1961 on when she began, for the first time, to use speech as an effective means of communication. The opportunities for intensive relationships with members of the nursing staff seemed to be a major factor in the consistency of her improvement.

After a while I got so close to her I was able to say: "I'm going to be angry with you. It won't be fun for us to be together, you can try me to the point where I am just discouraged." I'd use words like that about my feelings. And I'd say: "I have to be with you until it is time for me to leave, and I have to sit with you, but I don't have to like it."

There were times when she'd show a good sense of humor—little jokes about "bee's knees, and little legs down to here" and jokes about the body. Then she'd come up to me and say, "I'm happy, I'm happy."

She had begun to talk about her feelings, e.g. "I felt sad this afternoon and I felt like pounding and hitting. Miss M held me close and I did feel better." Her mental condition and social adjustment had improved, she was now more accessible to suggestion, more cooperative but still grossly disturbed.

What I always felt about Dora, after I heard about her illness when Jean was eight months old, and not able to touch her mother, yet able to see her, was that there has always been a double message to Jean: there, there it is – but you can't have it. That's when all the pillow fetish started.

I used to stare at Jean and fantasize what she'd be like if she were normal, and I always felt that she'd be nervous and wiry and busy, a smoker. I always felt she had so much potential, it was such a human waste.

She was well-formed and good-looking. Jean in contrast to the others on the ward had a very intelligent face. She also had excellent muscle tone, whereas the others were slack. She said a lot of things to people, but a lot of it was missed, because she would be deliberately obscure.

The staff working with Jean used to have to put her in seclusion, lock her in because she'd bang and scratch. One time she kept yelling, "What time is it?" I kept telling her the time and being real concrete about it and she'd say, "Tomato shaker what time is it, tomato shaker red?"

Jean had her period, and that's how she was telling me. What she was really saying was, "If you really love me and if you really care, you'll understand any old dumb thing I say to you, in other words, follow me."

Over the years I got to understand a lot of that. Tomato shaker red – it's red – it's that time of month. What time is it means I just got my period and I'm upset, have cramps and a headache. She didn't say any of that, just said "tomato shaker red" and "what time is it," and went absolutely crazy because I didn't get it. If I did, she'd have this funny way with her mouth (a whistling sound) and she'd smile behind her fingers.

Rages did not occur out of the blue but were precipitated by a lot of compulsive behavior, she worked herself up. I could see when it was going to happen. The factors were double meanings to things and not responding to her requests.

Every time Jean wanted something there was a huge effort to get her *everything she wanted. Once it was mustard spoons; she would get them and throw them out the window. You were responding to the concrete thing of what she was saying yet that really was not what she was saying. What she was saying was "get me something, bring me something."*

Once Jean went through a big screaming tantrum and all of a sudden she said, "I'm not going to go to the university." It just came out of her mouth: "I'm not going to school, I'm not going to be like you. I'm not going to be normal, I'm not going to have it. I've lost that opportunity."

These words came out of the blue and I responded with: "It's really sad, Jean, because underneath all of these things you'd like to be just like us with jobs and not have to be put into institutions." And then she cried.

Times like that when she and I were talking, her face was so relaxed, I felt very close to her, but I couldn't make the lifelong commitment to take care of her. I was interested in Jean's prior history and what Erikson observed, but I couldn't figure out how Jean had gotten so crazy.

I see now that perhaps she didn't

have the strength from the start, there was something wrong from birth. She had the best available in hospital treatment and psychotherapy at Langley Porter, yet she hadn't outgrown her problems. Therapy should have worked if it was going to.

EVEN THOUGH SHE WAS in her twenties, Jean remained on the children's ward for the duration of her stay at Langley Porter. She stayed on the ward in part because of her small frame and immaturity, but also because of the unusual circumstance that her mother was in treatment with two of the most senior psychiatrists in Children's Services.

For the two doctors, this was an unusual opportunity to pursue a lengthy psychotherapeutic program consistent with their clinical interest in childhood disorders, and to work with one of the most disturbed children they had ever seen.

Dora believed it was a terrible mistake that their therapy had not included their son, Mark. He needed desperately to talk to someone about his fears, anger, and apprehension, the repression of which had severely marred his personal growth. At the time, however, family therapy as we know it today, was not practiced. It was considered an innovative treatment and the two doctors seeing Jean and her parents were frequently criticized for using this approach.

Both of Jean's doctors agreed that her prospects for independent living were poor even though her progress at Langley Porter had been encouraging and rewarding. She acted out less and seemed responsive in a positive way to the steady, caring atmosphere created and maintained on the wards by staff and especially by the two staff nurses who cared for her.

Jean was finally discharged when the ward was changed to accommodate only very young children. The more aggressive and acting-out patients were being discharged to state hospitals—Jean's destination as well.

On the day of her discharge, the staff threw her a gigantic party. They gave her presents; it was like Christmas and her birthday rolled into one. Dora said the nicest gift was an address book with everybody's name and address in it. Jean was smiling and happy, as if she were going off to school.

But there was no school. She would go directly to Napa State Hospital.

Dora recalled that signs of hope in all directions had vanished. The doctors at Langley Porter were no longer going to try to help her. "They never actually said, 'We have done everything we possibly could do,' but that was their attitude." Dora expected Jean would be in the state hospital for the rest of her life. The doctors agreed that Jean would not get better.

Dora related that eight years before Jean went to Napa, she'd had the following anguished dream, which she now interpreted as a premonition of eventual state hospitalization, a future that she had dreaded:

I lay in bed facing a hill where there is a graveyard. I find it depressing always to see gravestones, all of children and so close, like in my backyard. I will turn my bed around and sleep the other way. I quarrel with Aron because something awful has happened. I refuse to become paralyzed…I am bitter. We do nothing. Why get continually upset?

They are to move the children's coffins and replace them with others. A man with a carload of new coffins is rolling them one after the other to be placed in now-open graves. I wonder if he does this carelessly and note with relief that he rolls them gently and smoothly. I look at the coffins now close to me. I have less horror than I thought to have.

I hear the bell ringing: "blow by north, the bell, blow by south, the bell, peace for all, the bell." I wake with a headache.

Quarrel is in my mind, the oppressive sense of long, drawn-out wars—useless wars—and a simple chant goes around in my head, and I find myself singing it to myself long after I'm awake: "My long, drawn-out years of useless war."

Chapter 9

Napa State Hospital

JEAN'S PARENTS DROVE HER to the state hospital, a two-hour trip from where they lived. They decided that they would bring her home every other weekend. This became their routine for the next three years.

The admission process only reinforced Dora's anxiety about the hospital:

> We were seen right away because no one else was being admitted at the time. The whole experience was weird. The doctor who saw us was an old crazy, a psychiatrist of course. They put him in this spot, I am sure, because he couldn't do much damage.
>
> He came out like a mad psychiatrist and said wildly, "Who is this patient?" Without listening, he grabbed Jean and

took her into his office. A moment later he poked his head out and said, "Who are you?" Then the maze of filling out forms, and it was decided that she would be a voluntary patient, and could sign herself out.

Dora's concern eased slightly when she saw the admission ward itself. The windows had curtains on them. There were small rooms with four beds and bedside tables next to each. The social worker was quick to tell her that registered nurses ran this ward, which was not the case on other wards.

Dora had arranged Jean's admission for a Thursday so that she would not have to wait long to go home on the weekend. However, they were informed that no one could leave for the first two weeks. Dora pleaded and explained they had arranged it this way because Jean would be easier to handle if she knew she'd be going home in two days.

The doctor assured Dora they had a way of dealing with miscreants. Dora responded that Jean was not a miscreant, that they wanted to avoid making her feel abandoned. He finally consented and promised to put a note on her chart. When Dora arrived on Saturday, there was no note on the chart. But Dora talked her way past everyone and secured Jean's release for the weekend.

When Dora found out later that there were sixty-five people on the ward, she was horrified. "At Langley Porter there had been a one-to-one relationship of staff to patient. However, compared to what happened later, this wasn't bad."

When Jean came home on weekends, Dora hired students who were happy to take Jean out on Saturday afternoons. Dora felt she herself couldn't do anything "fun" with her daughter. She couldn't take her to restaurants or stores because she still felt embarrassed by Jean's behavior. Jean enjoyed the lively presence of the students, who took her boating and to the tennis courts. Without their stimulation, she would withdraw and lie on her bed.

One weekday, Audrey, one of Jean's companions, drove to Napa to take Jean out on the hospital grounds. On her return, she called Dora, greatly agitated because Jean had been moved. She'd had a hard time locating her and said the new location was awful. Dora's heart sank; she knew immediately that what she had feared had happened. Jean had been transferred to the back ward.

That weekend, Dora and Aron went to pick Jean up and were sent to the far end of the grounds to a building with endless halls where Dora and Aron wandered confusedly from one part to another.

"It was right next to a big quarry and there was a cloud of dust in the air all the time," Dora said.

Arriving at last at ward 17, Jean's new location, Dora noticed that the pleasant features of the admission ward were absent. "The long halls were absolutely bare. The door to the Admission ward had been open, but this door was locked and you had to ring."

She and Aron waited with another family for the door to be unlocked. Through a peephole Dora saw people wandering around, looking just as she'd imagined those in a mental hospital would look.

"These people were crazy, whereas those in the admission ward didn't look very sick. On the surface their behavior was not different from the norm. When I reported this to Dr. Szurek back at Langley Porter, he said that anyone who has ever worked with disturbed children like Jean never sees anyone else as being very sick."

When Jean appeared, it was obvious she'd been heavily drugged. The nurse explained that Jean had been flipping the lights on and off at night, turning the television on and off, and in general spoiling the environment for the other patients. She'd been given a shot of Thorazine (an antipsychotic) to quiet her.

On her next visit to ward 17, Dora waited

about twenty minutes after ringing for entrance. Again, Jean was obviously dazed and medicated. Dora wasn't surprised that Jean was given a shot if she hadn't behaved. But she was astonished that, as a parent, she was not allowed on the ward. Especially since she'd done some checking on hospital conditions prior to Jean's admission and had heard that marvelous changes had taken place there, and how civilized the ward had become.

The truth, Dora said, is that "this was the back ward, the snake pit. Jean was at last in a state hospital, where they don't try. They abandon you."

But not everyone had abandoned Jean. At Langley Porter, she had been under the care of a dedicated staff of idealistic and caring nurses, and some of them visited Jean at Napa on their days off. Nurse M in particular visited Jean over many months after her admission. She reported:

> When Jean was placed at Napa I went up there to see her a lot. I don't know how it happened that they let me in there, 17, the back ward. I wasn't finished with her, didn't think I should stop there. I remember going up to Napa and seeing what she had to put up with.
>
> When I walked in the ward Jean came tearing towards me saying, "I want to get out of here, these people are crazy."

It was so clear. They were so crazy that
she stepped out of her craziness.

Nurse M's attitude was a reflection of Szurek's training at Langley Porter: she felt that a lot of Jean's craziness was put on because it was expected and allowed—intimating that the parents were somehow cueing Jean's disordered behavior.

Several weekends in a row, Dora asked to see where her daughter slept, but the nurses refused her request. One nurse said Dora was not allowed on the ward for her own safety, which conjured terrible visions that the ward was not safe for Jean, either. Little by little Dora found out what it was like inside:

> *There were 115 women on the ward, all ages, but not many young. Only psychiatric technicians were in charge of care. The doctor for this ward was responsible for two other wards also, 345 people in all. They slept 25 in a dormitory, and there were no bedside tables, patients had no access to their things. There was no place to put anything that was yours.*
>
> *A patient became depersonalized, and this was reflected in how the patient's relatives were treated. They too were depersonalized.*

Hospital personnel showed no interest in Dora and never asked her about Jean. "They didn't think that parents had anything to offer that would be of interest to them."

On the advice of Szurek, Dora asked to speak to the doctor in charge of Jean's ward. Instead of listening to what Dora had to say, the doctor lectured her on Jean's condition. Szurek himself visited the doctor, who gave him the same lecture and reassured both Szurek and Dora that he did not want Jean to receive shock treatments. Dora requested his statement in writing.

In response to Dora's complaint that she was not permitted to see the ward, the doctor in charge encouraged her to visit on a Wednesday to see the "program." The following Wednesday Dora was allowed on the ward:

> There was nothing hideous about it. It was just ghastly plain and very depressing. What struck me first was a round trough with spigots where the patients washed. In the middle of the hall was a glass "cubbyhole"—the nurses' station, where they stayed as much as possible and, understandably for them, probably tried never to come out.
>
> When I saw where Jean slept, I felt terrible. With no table to put her letters

on, Jean carried everything around with her all the time, all her precious belongings. Everything was locked up She could not get her toothbrush without asking.

The "program" that the doctor invited me to observe consisted of a volunteer dance teacher who came once a week and tried to get people on their feet and moving in some way. Most people sat in apathy, too medicated to respond. The line the doctor gave me was that things are so much better now than before tranquilizers, when it was a madhouse with screaming and yelling. The doctor just didn't know what a program was. The only program that was going on was tranquilizers.

One day the psychiatric technician on the ward told Dora her story. She loved her job doing motivational therapy with the patients, and the plan called for a daily group. But the technician said she never had time for a group because so much else needed to be done. A technician's tasks included separating and distributing medications for 115 people three to five times a day, essentially running a pharmacy for the ward. Dora believed these were good intentions, but the only place where a program of supervised activities like games and singing was carried out was on the admission ward, and Jean had been written off from the start because on that ward nobody was really sick.

Perhaps because Dora was the mother of a radically disturbed child, she found it hard to empathize with mentally ill adults who did not have Jean's kind of troubled history. She thought they should just "buck up and cut that out. They are not crazy," she said. "On the back ward, people are crazy, quite definitely crazy." All this was a shock to Dora. Her premise was that no person should be neglected and given up on, and that the hospital's goal should have been to aim for a positive treatment outcome and not throw people away.

As Dora related her story, I could feel the depth of her anguish and despair.

On the back ward Jean was kept medicated. On weekends her face was mask-like and she hardly spoke. At home, she refused to take her pills.

Nurse M advised Jean to take the medication:

> *Jean was so unreasonable. I told her that if you refuse your medication they are going to give it to you in the butt, and she refused it orally for whatever reason and she had abscesses all over her butt, but they didn't care. I was so mad at her because I knew she had to adjust.*

> *I think we finally talked her into it,*
> *and told her that they were going to give*
> *it to her and nobody liked the way she*
> *acted. They were not going to put up with*
> *it, and nobody cares that much up there,*
> *that's the truth. I think she hated herself*
> *and thought she had to be punished and*
> *thought that she was nothing.*

Although Dora reported to the nurse in charge that Jean had agreed to take her medication orally, the nurse refused to change to pills. Dora asked the nurses to give Jean a chance, but they said they were too busy. She felt they didn't care, but at the same time she recognized the pressure they were under and how they could become hardened to the suffering and insanity. "They care only so they can live through their shift," she said.

Nurse M also reported the following, which likely would not have happened anywhere except on the back ward:

> *Jean made one friend on 17, a black*
> *woman who had killed two of her chil-*
> *dren. She loved and mothered Jean,*
> *brushed her hair and looked after her,*
> *and Jean loved her too.*
> *Jean also knew how to make people*

angry. On the ward she would switch the light on and off. One time a patient asked her to stop and she did not. She was almost choked to death as a result but fortunately somebody saved her in time.

She lay on her bed—almost black from being choked. But I knew how mean and deliberate she could be and she almost did that to herself—asked for it—I think she could control things. But there you are, at Napa. I'll bet she slipped way back, way back.

After six months, Jean's medication had been doubled from what it was at admission. The dosage had been increased as her body became immune to the effects. Due to the increase, her behavior was subdued and she was transferred to the County ward. It was smaller, only 85 patients, but with no other noticeable difference.

Chapter 10
Death of Jean's Father

URING JEAN'S HOSPITALIZATION at Napa, Dora's home life was difficult. She worked full-time as a librarian. If she worked on a Saturday, she would go to the hospital on Sunday just to visit for the day. By the weekend she was worn out from working and running the household. Aron couldn't help because of his health.

Aron had been seriously ill from 1960 on. He had suffered a prostate operation and, soon after, a stomach ulcer. His bones were brittle from osteoporosis. He broke one arm, then the other. He smoked incessantly, his hands were palsied, and there was no way to reform his unhealthy eating habits. Bread, cake, and meat were his primary foods. He would overeat and then experience violent stomach pains.

In the summer of 1966, at the age of 71,

he collapsed. His blood pressure reached zero; he hovered between life and death for a week, then died. His death certificate stated the cause of death as emphysema and renal failure. As far as Dora was concerned, for twelve years she had earned her own living while caring for two chronic patients, Jean and Aron. Once he was gone, she felt a sense of relief.

Jean knew from the weekend visits that her father was gravely ill. His health had steadily declined while she was in the hospital. Two days after his death, Dora went to pick up Jean. When told that her father had died, she repeated this fact over and over, as though uncomprehending and unbelieving. But otherwise she seemed unaffected.

Dora took Jean to see a former therapist at Langley Porter. In his office Jean lay on the couch in silence and without reaction while the doctor tried to encourage her to express her feelings. The next day she complained of a toothache. Dora took her to the dentist, who injected her gum and filled her tooth. Dora knew, as they were leaving the office, that something else was wrong with her. She had a mask-like expression and her demeanor was lifeless. She refused food and didn't speak.

Dora expected Jean's strange behavior to disappear, as usual, but the next morning Jean sat motionless and refused to eat. Dora grew alarmed.

Late that afternoon Jean spoke. She asked Dora to fix the glove compartment. The door to the glove compartment in the car had been jammed for weeks. Dora leaped at this request and they drove to see Tom at a local car repair shop.

Tom had been one of Jean's first companions many years earlier. He'd had a special rapport with Jean because he genuinely liked her and could be both gentle and strong. Dora and Jean had not seen Tom for ten years.

He fixed the glove compartment and Jean seemed relieved. He took them for a ride, treating Jean as he had always done, and she came out of her catatonic-like stupor.

From then on she seemed all right. It is possible that when the vital thread of her father's life was severed, a token of continuity from the past, especially from a man who had been close to her, was of special significance.

Jean stayed at home for a while because of her father's death and eventually went back to Napa and stayed for another year.

BY THE WINTER OF 1967, conditions at the hospital had deteriorated due to drastic budget cuts for mental health care, as mandated by the California legislature. When Dora drove Jean back to the hospital on Sunday nights, there would be only one technician on the ward, sometimes a male, in charge of eighty-five women. Her medication had now been tripled from her dosage at admission.

That spring, a social worker friend of Dora's neighbor went to visit Jean at Napa and decided, after spending some time with her, that Jean could possibly live in more normal surroundings among people outside of the hospital. After much struggle with the hospital personnel, who did not believe Jean could make the switch to community living, Dora received a skeptical approval.

Release from the hospital, however, was contingent on the hospital applying and receiving approval for Supplemental Security Income (SSI) on Jean's behalf, and on Dora finding a place for her to live.

At this point Dora began skipping Jean's medication when she was at home. When Jean came home for a ten-day visit, Dora cut the dose to almost nothing and said Jean came to life during those ten days.

Back at the hospital, however, the attendants had a terrible time trying to control Jean and she was denied leave privileges for the following weekend. Upon hearing their refusal, she swiftly piled all the furniture in the middle of the room, almost to the ceiling, and climbed on it, making everyone afraid she would fall. She went home on the weekend.

It occurs to me now, as I write this, that many of us living within accepted norms of behavior, must take the long way around—sometimes for years—to make ourselves understood, while Jean's maneuver forced the issue speedily.

In the meantime, the social worker was having trouble finding a place for Jean. The hospital balked at applying for SSI, and two hospital psychiatrists as well as the head technician on the floor advised against Jean's leaving. They told Dora that the way she could help Jean most was by giving her the prescribed medication, and maybe after some years she would be ready for psychotherapy.

It was obvious to Dora that these professionals did not know Jean's complicated history. No one at the hospital had ever asked Dora about it, which had consistently left her feeling devastated. She was relentless and persisted despite her frustration to persuade the hospital to apply for SSI on Jean's behalf. In the spring of 1967 Jean was released. She had been at Napa for three years.

PART III
Significant Changes

Chapter 11

A Community
of Friends

IN THE ABSENCE OF A PLACE for Jean to live in the community, she would live at home. Dora found Sylvia, a former family caretaker, to come and take care of her daily during the week. Dora hired two companions to take Jean out on weekends. "I had already been working with two girls since 1962 when Jean was at Langley Porter and would come home on weekends. They took full responsibility and did everything without me."

When Sylvia moved out of the area after a month, Dora placed an ad at the university for students to work as companions. She deliberately did not seek people studying psychology or social work. She'd hired such people in the past, but they had been a complete failure, she said, in that they felt superior and wanted to psychoanalyze Jean or not bother with her at all. Dora's ad read: "Help needed for mentally ill female. Acts like a child but is much older."

Respondents to her ad included many art, nursing, and physical education majors. The athletic types had a certain calm about them, Dora said. They felt secure in their bodies and could teach Jean swimming, take her bicycling, and engage her in other physical activities. Art majors had the same calm and involved Jean in the expressive arts without expectation or criticism.

Jean was still difficult. In the street she would run away from whomever she was with, kick walls, walk up to strangers, sniff them, and tell them they smelled. If she saw a dog coming in the distance she would climb on the roof of the nearest car in terror. However, the companions Dora hired had a certain fearlessness about trying new things. They weren't afraid of Jean. Most significant was that being with them made Jean feel accepted.

Dora slowly came to realize that Jean would never have to go back to Napa or to another hospital, and as we talked a huge smile crossed her face as she recalled the immense relief she had felt at that knowledge:

> *After Jean had been home about three months it began to seep through my brain that I wasn't feeling down as I had expected I would feel. We were completely on our own. Langley Porter was*

out; we couldn't go back there. I realized that I had great confidence, and I began to feel, hardly daring to admit it to my consciousness, that what we were doing was working with her.

We were thrown on our own, so what did we do? We hired untrained girls as companions and the assignment was to undertake things that were "fun." Soon they were doing all kinds of things, like embroidery and crafts. In effect we started plain teaching and training.

Although the psychoanalytic inter-pretations of why she kissed the ground or did this or that were always unanswered questions, they were quickly swept aside, into teaching and training. That's all we had to offer, and I think it was rather worth it. I was absolutely in ecstasy.

I simply couldn't believe it. I was taken out of jail, is the only way I can say it.

After what we had been through, this was so marvelous and we were very happy. We didn't have any violence during this whole time. No rages, no assaults.

The first companions I hired stayed for several years. They were the so-called "flower children" of the mid-sixties and they accepted Jean into their group. They had an attitude of generosity, of loving and giving, of taking care of everybody. For years after, many of the companions that had been hired stayed in touch with me and told me they were still influenced by their work with Jean. They had taken her to restaurants and they had watched her behave oddly. It was not looked upon as being so terrible, because odd things were not that conspicuous in the late 1960's and early '70s.

Jean was absorbed into the life of these girls, their boyfriends, husbands, and children. She was assimilated into their culture. They picked her up and carried her into the mainstream with them. Treating her normally really seemed to help her.

Dora always emphasized to Jean's companions that they never had to do anything they did not feel comfortable with. Allowing them a certain freedom was a lesson Dora had learned at Langley Porter about her own relationship with Jean. There, the therapeutic team had never pressed Dora to do more than she could. Dora told Jean's companions there was nothing they could do that would permanently mar Jean's situation.

They were encouraged to tell Dora what they could and could not handle. All the lessons she had learned through her own experience and therapy were put into practice.

Dora related an incident that Sara, one of Jean's companions, had shared with her:

> *Sara took Jean into a variety store. Jean hastily grabbed a doll (the kind that "wets") and dashed out of the store and into a coffee shop next door. There she grabbed a cup of coffee out of someone's hands and poured it down the doll's throat. All the while everyone involved was in mad chase after her. Sara quickly placated the astonished customer and store owner, firmly placed Jean in the car, and drove to the yacht harbor, where amidst the din of the wind and waves Sara yelled as loudly as she could. Jean could see that she was broken up about what had happened, and became remorseful and quiet.*

This bizarre experience reminded Sara to remain aware and cautious on future outings. It is possible Jean was testing limits with Sara and also that she actually felt Sara's remorse and sadness.

Dora admitted that she had a certain anxiety

about the drugs the people she'd hired might have been using, especially marijuana. "I took it up with them, saying I didn't care what they did, but I felt they would be very sorry if they got Jean into 'something.' And that never happened."

She explained that she always tried to understand Jean and to do what she thought was best in any situation. In retrospect she realized that in trying to help a situation she could be misunderstood, and agitate her. For example:

> One day I took her to the university campus near where we lived, and wanted her to do some running. She chose a grassy place and instead of running around the edge, she ran around in a little circle. I said, "That won't do," and she said, "I ran a lot. I ran a lot, I did run a lot." I said, "You cheated yourself, you have to run around the edge." She ran around the edge twice and said, "I ran around a lot." I said, "You ran around twice." She came back to me during the day saying over and over, "I ran a lot." And I would say, "Two times. Not a little, not a lot. It's two times."

When they arrived at the car, Jean raised her foot to kick her mother, but didn't. When they got home, Jean physically attacked Dora, and Dora knew it was because she had told Jean she had not run very far.

In another incident, Jean was not ready for bed and went into her room to sew without turning on the light. Dora said, "You can't sew in there. If you must sew, sew where there is light, turn the lamp on." Jean said, "Don't turn the lamp on."

It seems to me that Jean fought her mother's control meaningfully in this incident, with less resistance, and it came through when she said, "Don't turn the lamp on." A normal person might have added "and leave me alone."

Jean's compulsions increased noticeably after such interactions. Dora was thoughtful about the incidents and the ensuing reactions and tried to avoid this kind of confrontation.

Chapter 12
Autism Begins to Be Recognized

ONE OF THE MOST significant outgrowths of the human potential movement of the 1960's and 70's was an increased awareness and acceptance of individuals with mental and physical disabilities. However, early infantile autism was still virtually unheard of, even though Kanner had identified it in 1943.

In 1956, psychologist Bernard Rimland had become the father of an autistic child.[16] The birth of his son started a chain of events that proved to be of great benefit to autistic people and their families. He made an intensive study of the literature on autism and posited the theory that autism was an organic disorder and not a consequence of parental rejection.

Dora read Rimland's book, *Early Infantile Autism*, published in 1964, and her reactions were mostly negative. Although she had gained much

118

insight from her time in therapy, she still resisted the idea that Jean might have an organic problem.

In general, Dora said, his book angered her. She responded similarly to the way she'd responded to Kanner's article 20 years earlier: by denying the suggestion of "innate disturbance" as basic to Jean's disorder. Her belief at that time had been, "My child is perfect."

She recalled a conversation with Erikson, in which he remarked that parents of intellectually disabled children are not guilty, and Jean appeared to be intellectually disabled. Dora had rejected his suggestion. He was amazed and said that parents of intellectually disabled children should consider that they are not guilty.

Reading Rimland, Dora felt confused, in that she believed she was not to blame for Jean's condition, yet she was not able to accept Rimland's theory of biogenicity.

Rimland had tried for years to locate Jean and her family, and in 1970 he found them and came to visit. Dora liked him and since 1967 had been in agreement with his biogenetic stance on infantile autism, which she had finally accepted as Jean's condition. Jean was thirty-six at the time and had been away from the hospital for six years.

Dora had finally changed her view because after Napa she had begun to observe Jean more objectively. She'd noted that some of Jean's behaviors had remained more or less unchanged since early childhood, while others had become less apparent.

When Dora met Rimland, she was in her mid-sixties. According to Erikson's theory of the "Eight Stages of Man" described in *Childhood and Society*, the older-age phase, which he named "Ego Integrity," brings with it a basic acceptance of one's life as having been inevitable, given the forward and back of decisions made or not made, with a minimum of regret and blame. Erikson called the final ego strength of the life cycle "Wisdom."

It is possible that Dora, in her older-age phase, was seeking to defend with dignity what no longer could be denied—an organic basis for Jean's condition.

During our taping session, Dora expressed again the emotional significance of facing what she could no longer deny—the agony of realizing she was the mother of an abnormal child. She leaned forward, and in a dry voice said:

> *In the biological sense, part of the whole biology is reproduction, raising another being that will take your place. This is a fundamental, animal biological fact. You can't, like birds do, toss the fractured ones out of the nest and forget about them, so that it stands—as a*

failure...that I haven't done that perfectly simple thing that any fool could do. You don't have to be bright or go to college or have money. Anybody can reproduce... and you can't. I don't believe it was something that I did; I believe now that it was there at birth.

In accepting the endogenous nature of Jean's condition, Dora released herself from blame. From that point forward, she had reflected on new directions emerging in the etiology and treatment of mental illness. For example, in 1975 the National Society for Autistic Children published information from a federal task force, which had appeared in the Washington Post, stressing an important change that had been occurring over the past twenty-five years: biomedical research indicated that some forms of mental illness that were due to a biomedical cause could respond to medical (drug) treatment. The article also pointed out that mental health research and treatment techniques had not reached a point where mental health problems could be considered solved, nor could treatments that are considered effective be accepted as "cures." Importantly, it indicated that environment plays a major role in the exacerbation of mental illness.

SPARKED BY OUR ONGOING interview sessions, which by then had gone on for several months, and by Dora's heightened interest in this subject, she and I decided to attend the 1977 annual meeting of the National Society for Autistic Children in San Francisco.

Writers, researchers, parents, children—all were present. Dora saw with relief and delight that she was no longer alone in her struggle.

The meeting engendered an atmosphere of supportiveness and sharing. Parents of young autistic children expressed what Dora had learned from many years of heartrending experience: that most communities had no facilities for the care or education of these children. Like Dora, many parents had spent a small fortune obtaining a diagnosis, only to learn that no further help was available.

Dora's weathered, compassionate face had a staying kind of beauty. In it I saw an old warrior still.

Chapter 13

Benefits of a New Treatment

I N THE EARLY 1970'S Dora developed an interest in a new, non-punitive treatment for positive change in autistic people, based on behavior modification. Although behavior modification was not a new idea, in the 1970's Ivar Lovaas, a Norwegian-American clinical psychologist, developed a specialized technique using this method to successfully modify the inappropriate behavior of autistic individuals through teaching.[17]

Critics of the Lovaas method suggested that the long-range value of this technique might depend either on reengineering the home environment or on asking parents to give up their personal activities. They would then devote entire days to teaching conformity via delivering or withholding positive reinforcements for their child's behavior. Also, because the relationship between parent and child is beset with subtle feelings and manipulations, where would the parent take the overflow of their feelings that were not part of the behavior modification exchange between parent and child? This treatment modality also assumed parents' mental health and stability. Who would monitor the behavior of the parent?

Dora was initially repelled by the thought of behavior modification as a treatment for Jean. It was totally different from any approach she was used to. Her therapist at Langley Porter had focused on feelings and basic motivations, whereas behavior modification worked with what could be observed and readily manipulated.

Nevertheless, she had been corresponding for several years with Clara Parks, mother of an autistic daughter and author of a novel, *The Siege,* based on her daughter Jill's life. Behavior modification had been very helpful in changing Jill's behavior through the use of positive and negative reinforcement strategies. Dora gradually became interested and decided to try it with Jean.

She began with an exclusively positive approach. Meeting with a few of Jean's companions, they all decided that Jean's whining and her terror of dogs would be good behaviors to eliminate or at least modify. The reward would be money, and Jean was interested. At first she was rewarded hourly for not whining, then at half-day intervals. Her whining was dramatically reduced after a few days and did not return to its previous level.

Dora taught all of Jean's companions the new strategy of reward and punishment. One of them would say to Jean, "When you come to a dog, say hello and smile." Jean was finally able to walk down the street without becoming wild and agitated at the sight of a dog. "In this way," Dora said, "some of her more disturbing social habits decreased markedly and some of them almost entirely. Jean learned self-control and how to behave from the simple use of behavior modification." Dora wanted to learn more about this technique.

In 1975 she heard about the Family Resource Development Agency, which provided families with a parent consultant who would arrange an individualized behavior modification program based on the child's needs. The goal was to assist parents in becoming self-reliant in the process of changing undesirable behaviors in their children. The objectives were to eliminate the need for institutionalization; develop the child's abilities in language, self-help, and social skills that would make possible a semi-independent adult life; and encourage a positive attitude in parents toward their difficult child.

Dora questioned whether Noel, the parent consultant assigned to her, would be willing and able to work with a 40-year-old "child."

He was willing to try, and after their initial

consultation Dora was eager for the service. Noel helped her develop effective strategies for working with Jean, and Dora described a representative example:

> I told Jean to "sit down and do your embroidery." She got up and moved around the room. Noel said, "Your mother told you to sit down." Jean did not sit down. Noel gently placed her in the chair and said, "You have to sit there for five minutes before you can get up." Jean got up immediately. He again placed her in the chair. Each time she stood up, he added one minute until she had to sit for twenty-five minutes, which she finally did. After the time had passed, Noel praised her and said, "You can do your embroidery now."

Dora was amazed and pleased. Jean's responsiveness to Noel's commands were reminiscent of how Jean had tended to cooperate in the past if she was treated gently but firmly and directly.

By practicing the skills Noel taught her, Dora learned how to avoid getting overly involved with Jean's problem and how to maintain an objective stance when Jean assaulted her.

Another application of this method was to

post a list of Jean's expected behaviors on the wall and check it at mid-day and again at night. The reward for the expected behavior was money. From this practice, Jean learned about money— how to spend it, what "change" meant, and how to deposit it at a bank.

Although Jean did not understand the meaning of money, Dora felt that learning about it gave Jean a feeling of achievement. Eventually money was phased out and colored stars and praise sufficed as rewards. Dora gained tremendous strength from knowing she could handle Jean with some objectivity, which allowed her to feel more relaxed in Jean's presence.

Dora shared another powerful example of her success with behavioral techniques. For many years she had gone to bed fearing that Jean might wake up during the night and disturb her. Noel suggested that Dora lock her bedroom door at night. After telling Jean that the door would be locked, Dora followed through and actually locked it.

As a result, Jean's rituals—which included rushing up and down the stairs in a frenzy around 3 A.M., switching on the vacuum cleaner, repeatedly opening and closing the refrigerator door— stopped entirely. Dora said with relief, "For the first time in years I went to sleep knowing that I would not be disturbed. When I am rested I can handle everything so much better. Things are so good between us now."

Encouraged by Noel, Dora began to demonstrate more predictability and decisiveness with Jean. She no longer felt victimized by feelings of inadequacy in handling her and could also express loving feelings more openly:

> One night at bedtime Jean made her usual request to "sit with me" before going to sleep. I sat on her bed and she began playfully making fun with words like "reh-eh" (rectum) and "mastercut" (masturbate). I asked laughingly what the words meant and Jean responded with mischievous glee, "Why, they're neologisms of course," having been told at the hospital that this term described her style of using words. I sat with Jean in playful exchange, and she slipped her hand out from under her pillow, reached for my hand, and pressed it. This was the first time in her life she had done that—reached out to me. It was a gratifying moment.

As Dora recounted this, her face was smiling, relaxed, and full of feeling.

MY INTERVIEWS WITH DORA ended in late summer of 1978, and I went back to my own life. When I returned to visit in 1980, Jean had just come back from an outing with a companion and her face lit up when she greeted me. She appeared only slightly older, with a bright and happy demeanor.

Dora filled me in on Jean's treatment and progress. She had been learning new skills and had made some of her own clothes. She had also been painting with as much brilliance as she once showed in music. "When she can do things like that," said Dora, "there is a great flowering from her." Taking me to her room, Jean calmly and with genuine pride showed me a collection of handsome pendants, necklaces, rings, and other beautifully handcrafted items she had made. Her focused attention astounded me. Any sign of the frustration that used to cause her to fly into a rage was absent. In her closet she showed me a handsomely embroidered dress she had recently finished. On her bed was a knitted blanket in progress.

I took her hands, now open and relaxed, and said, "Jean, you make beautiful things with your hands." "Yes," she replied, "I am a craftsman."

Profoundly impressed with Jean's progress, I wanted to know how it had all come about, and sat down to chat with Dora. Jean joined us with her knitting and counted stitches out loud, but softly, to herself. While Dora and I talked, Jean interrupted to ask for something and then said, "It doesn't do any good to whine. I'm not interrupting"—both parroted statements, but appropriately used. Dora responded by agreeing that it did no good to whine and told her to hold off because she was interrupting. I was pleased to see that the climate between them had changed.

No longer intimidated or feeling guilty, Dora was taking a hard and straight line with her daughter, in a calm and relaxed manner. I remembered the "fits" of long ago, the screaming, whining, and clawing and how she had stood helpless and sad with little attempt to stay Jean's wild hands as they tore at her. I remembered Dora's scarred hands and arms. Now she was not anticipating a fit, and a fit did not occur. I was relieved to see the peaceful interaction between mother and daughter.

After Napa, when Jean was an adult and in the daily care of her companions, her autism had begun to disappear, and in two to three years it was vastly reduced. Dora said, "It was because of the new way we were treating her—much more like what I wanted all the time. People were paying attention to her and teaching her, not psychoanalyzing her."

I asked, "Do you think that if this treatment had been tried twenty years ago the effect would have been the same?" "I don't doubt it for a minute," she replied.

Not officially considered "treatment" at that time, the hiring of companions was successful because Dora hired people who saw Jean as an individual and who tuned in to her style of expressing what was of interest to her. Also, they modeled desirable behavior by example. Jean went along with them, and they discovered how much she could be taught and what they could offer.

It is possible that the hiring of companions worked well not only because Jean was accepted and not judged by them, but also because she was involved in the expressive arts, where no criticism or expectation was placed on her. She may also have been inspired by the creative possibilities of working with color, texture, and design.

Chapter 14

Dora Speaks Out

WITH JEAN IN AN agreeable situation at home, Dora felt more free to contribute to the growing interest and understanding of autism. It meant a lot to her to be able to use her experience and ideas to significantly improve the plight of the mentally ill, and she continued relentlessly to bring her voice to this movement.

Years before, in 1968, a year after Jean had come home from the state hospital, Dora had retired from library work and started to look for ways to make her ideas about autism heard. She had attended meetings of the National Mental Health Association, where she initially found the same prejudice she had seen in the professional world—a psychoanalytic approach to patients with Jean's condition.

Everyone on the Board of Directors was a psychiatrist, and they talked only about prevention,

Dora claimed, not about treatment of sick people.

She faithfully attended meetings and became acquainted with the association's policies. She found a lack of interest in hospital care and was advised by a social worker friend that she would have to fight, even get into politics herself if necessary, to make herself heard.

At the meetings Dora was a persistent and articulate spokesperson about treatment and care of autistic and other mentally ill people, and after a year she was invited to become a board member. One of her first jobs was to write a proposal requesting state funds to provide day care in halfway houses. The proposal described the plight of patients who, on being discharged from hospitals to the community, found no program available to help them and ended up being readmitted. The County Mental Health Association had refused to consider building a new hospital because they believed, as did Dora, that what was needed instead was other kinds of care in the community.

She also worked for the Lanterman-Petris-Short Act, which would provide more community services and get people out of hospitals.[18]

In 1970, Dora wrote a paper called "The Mental Health Aspects of Welfare," which she presented at a meeting of the California Mental Health Board.

Out of this paper grew an espousal for

advocacy training for mental health workers. A grant was obtained and volunteers were trained to act as liaison workers between mentally ill individuals and all the available community services. Dora also advocated for respite houses designed to give overnight relief to parents if they needed it. They could use this service for twenty-one days a year.

In 1977, Dora received the National Mental Health Association Volunteer of the Year Award and the sum of $1000. She gave the money in equal parts to the Berkeley Creative Living Center and to the Creative Growth Center. She was invited to Washington, D. C. to receive the award as a guest of the National Institute of Mental Health.

While in Washington, Dora was invited to testify before the Congressional Subcommittee on Welfare Reform. This is an excerpt from her statement to the committee:

> *I am the mother of a forty-three-year-old autistic woman who has been severely ill since her first year.*
>
> *After eighteen years in a state institution and in treatment for a period of twenty-eight years, she has been home for the last decade, receiving attendant care from students who provide teaching, exercise, recreation, and other activities*

not possible in a hospital situation.

I am concerned that training and rehabilitation services be available to all disabled persons who require it. I do not think the legislator or planner who casually recommends quarterly or annual reviews of disability understands how demoralizing they often are. For one thing, a change or disruption of ordinary routine and schedules, which to a normal person might be only an annoyance, for a mentally disabled person can be a fantastic threat, and can create unbearable anxiety. Even more serious is the necessity to reassert the painful fact of disability itself and the humiliating fact of one's dependency.

My next concern is with attendant care. I hope that funds will be included to provide adequate attendant care where necessary. In our case this assistance made all the difference between hospitalization and community living. Especially where there is no day care, proper attendant care can be the decisive factor in avoiding hospitalization.

When my daughter was young, they didn't know what her problem was. They made every diagnosis you could imagine.

135

There was no diagnosis which actually, at that point, was known. Every place we went, they said, "It's too bad, we can't help you." Today in California, education is mandated for these children until age twenty-one.

The following excerpt from an interview with Dora on the subject of burnout illustrates her empathy, intelligence, and continued willingness to reach out on behalf of other parents faced with a similar situation. The interview appeared in the *Journal of Autism and Developmental Disorder, Volume 9 #1, 1979.*

The burn-out syndrome seems to me to be an overwhelming discouragement. It undermines the most heroic efforts, and like a clinical depression, cripples one for the time being. There seems to be no direction in the flailing about. In the struggle to meet a continuous stream of crises. There is a breakdown in the ability to see such events in relation to the past history and the present efforts.

The key to preventing burn-out lies in respite.

But what kind of respite? Custodial care is certainly better than nothing. It can relieve a situation temporarily. But it leaves the parent with the nagging feeling that time is being wasted, and that tomorrow the same problem will be there facing us.

Perhaps burn-out would not occur if the child or adult were in a secure, ongoing program, that could provide work, creative arts and so on with no upper age limit. This should be a stimulating, vigorous program taking up most of the day. Parents would then have a genuine respite in which to restore their own energies, and carry on their own lives outside of the responsibilities for an autistic person.

Concomitantly, there would be practical training of parents and workers in handling day to day problems before they become crises. Sharing skills could encourage the worker or parent and help to develop his/her control of a situation.

Workers and parents should feel free to quit, without prejudice, when the going gets too tough.

This knowledge can help people not feel trapped. Easier said than done for parents, but I think that they must feel free and guilt-free about resigning the responsibility even if it is to a state hospital.

137

I would hate to see burn-out as an inevitable and incurable malady which strikes only the most dedicated. Like autism, I believe it can be conquered

One afternoon Dora and I sat outside her house in the hills overlooking the bay. Her face looked care-worn as she expressed her concern for Jean's future.

We discussed possibilities, and a unique concept began to form that would lead her into the next phase of her activism.

No existing facility or institution offered a satisfactory plan whereby Jean and others with similar long-term problems could live comfortably within a community. Dora organized a group of parents of autistic adults and together they began to forge a long-term residential plan, since ultimately all autistic children and adults require some form of long-term living arrangement.

The parents proposed a group of four or five houses, each with a maximum of three residents. One house would be a small urban farm and would look like other houses in the neighborhood rather than like an institution. The residents would raise their own vegetables and take care of their house.

The challenge for them would be to live and work in the community and support themselves in as normal a way as possible. The five houses would not have to be adjacent, but in the same general neighborhood, so residents could come together easily when they desired.

This unique plan conceived by Dora and the parents was significant because it offered the protection and support of a small, family-type community in which autistics seem to thrive.

It would also make it possible to deal with a wide range of abilities and handicaps that autistic adults exhibit. The plan would make it difficult or impossible to combine autistic adults with schizophrenics or individuals who are intellectually disabled. It would be very clear from their behavior that their needs were different.

The group believed that the cost of an urban farm program could be kept low. Dora explained: "The staff who would work there would not necessarily be trained in working with the mentally ill, but would have other skills and would be able to take responsibility as well as to empathize with some baffling people, and some experience with farming is essential.

Dora hoped to interest the Department of Housing and Urban Development (HUD) in financing all or part of this project. In addition, HUD might pay for the program by contacting the Social Service Bureau to provide the necessary care.

DURING THIS PERIOD WHEN the parents' group was planning the urban farm program, and Dora was becoming increasingly active in community mental health, Jean was slowly becoming more integrated into community life through outings with her companions. She seemed pleased with her daily life. Dora felt more pressed than ever to claim her own time and pay attention to parts of her life separate from Jean.

Jean's desire to be "close to mama" was not something she had expressed in prior years, but when Dora became more involved in her own pursuits, Jean began to express it directly. She said, "Upstairs, not close to you?" in response to having a downstairs bedroom away from Dora's room when Dora had decided that Jean would sleep downstairs rather than upstairs. "Sad," Dora said, "because I wished she wasn't that attached."

Dora wanted Jean to live in an independent residence so that she could "be at home when I want her and when she wants to be, and she can also have a separate life."

She researched options and was pleased to find one possibility where Jean could try to live away from home. She was conditionally accepted at Gateway House, a residential treatment center in Pacific Grove, California.[19] Dora liked their program, which included academic subjects and physical education. Jean, in her forties at the time, stayed for three months and then began attacking people. The school decided that she could not stay.

"If they had been willing to keep her I would have been very tempted to make it a permanent solution. However, she was away from home totally and she didn't want to be. She hadn't consented. It was simply heartbreaking to hear her say, "Not really? Not always? Not forever?" in response to being sent there."

This disappointment and Dora's failure to gain the respite she'd been seeking weighed heavily on her.

In a harsh whisper Dora said, "I could have done otherwise."

My insane optimism and efforts were to turn everything upside down in order to fit into her behavior. So was my refusal to give up trying to make it work at Langley Porter. I should never have gotten into this thing this far and this deep.

I could have done a thousand other things with my life, anything that I wanted to do. I never had the chance to pick and choose what I wanted to do with my life except for marriage—certainly not even that, if I stop and think about it. When I married, I had to have marriage, to have love and sex and all the rest of it. There was no woman's movement, no counseling—nobody thought of such things. You solved your own problems for better or worse.

**Upon the absolute reality of time
that wants exact change
from the bill of promise
you have made and bowed before,
bowed before.**

IN 1979, WHEN JEAN WAS forty-five, she joined the Berkeley Creative Living Center (renamed the Berkeley Creative Wellness Center in 2011).[20] This was an adult mental health day program based on the unique needs of the individuals who attended. Although not a residential plan, it seemed a good alternative at the time, and Jean appeared to thrive in this environment. Her behavior became less troublesome and she was noticeably happier and more responsive.

Dora believed these changes were due to her attendance at the Center. Rather than make her conform to an already existing program, the Center made allowances for her differences. They recognized that Jean worked better if she was permitted to work independently as much as possible.

This attitude on the part of others had worked well in the past for Jean with the nurses at the hospital and with her flower-children companions. Part of each day at the Center was spent assembling boxes, for which Jean got paid, and which she finished in less than half the time it took others. Instead of sitting and waiting for others to finish, she would go and get more supplies, an indication she was taking a certain amount of responsibility.

One of Jean's former companions, no longer able to spend time with her because of work commitments, would take her out for a few hours one evening a week, just because she liked Jean.

Dora was in her late seventies when she said. "When I see people really caring, I am not so worried about dying. The next thing is to continue to try and work out a residential plan."

At one point Dora said, "If only Aron was still alive to see Jean now. He was so sure that the state hospital would be the final alternative."

Due to Dora's continuous effort, Jean eventually moved willingly to residential housing operated by what is now called the East Bay Regional Center, in a nearby suburb.

Fortunately, mother and daughter were no longer forced by circumstance to be constantly together. Living apart gave Dora the freedom she desired—to have more of her own life—and allowed the hours she and Jean did spend together to be more rewarding.

DORA BECAME MORE REFLECTIVE about her total experience and life with Jean. She related that for more than eighteen years her family, with the exception of Mark, had received traditional psychoanalytic psychotherapy. Jean's condition had been viewed as a mental illness, and was treated primarily (from the 1940's through the early '60s) by psychotherapy. No residential facility or school or day program would take Jean. Langley Porter had held out hope that her condition could be cured or at least greatly ameliorated. Dora had accepted Langley Porter's solution to send Jean to the state hospital only when she felt that keeping her at home was destroying the whole family.

Dora began to summon up deep feelings that had been gathering for many years:

> *I felt that through therapy I had gained insight into my own methods of interaction with Jean. I was encouraged to express my feelings or at least to recognize them. I had held everything back, as did Aron, my husband, who found it unbearably hard to go into therapy—he*

didn't want to go—he felt humiliated by the experience.

It was hard for me to accept Jean's extreme behavioral abnormalities in part because I would have felt disloyal to Langley Porter. I felt too obligated. Always trying to adjust my critical feelings of them to my feelings of gratefulness to them. Jean was sent home from Napa having ingested a new drug. We were not told what she had been given this new prescription for, nor what kind of behavior to expect from it.

It's a marvelous rationalization, to lay blame on parents, when doctors can't do anything with a patient. Somebody's got to be at fault.

She said further that Jean had experienced kindness and consistency, however, from a variety of people—psychiatrists and nurses, as well as secretaries and maintenance crew, among others.

Dora had felt very successful in training and managing Jean's hired companions and learned not to put Jean into the care of anyone who found her difficult to handle. Out of despair and exhaustion, Dora had stopped demanding what people could not give. "I no longer made demands on anyone. Whatever came along that Jean would enjoy was okay. The present was the important consideration."

Gradually Dora had stopped feeling that all efforts on her daughter's behalf were a means to her cure. She began to see that that was all there was—there were no more normal measures for Jean and that's why having fun with her companions was okay. "I grew very strong and never complained when her companions couldn't come. I just managed, and in that way I got the best out of them."

With a steady gaze and in a quiet voice, Dora continued to talk about what she knew were severe but certain truths.

In nature, the survival of the fittest demands the rejection of the sick or deviant child. The survival of the individual mother demands it. Some families reject their deviant child and institutionalize them. Those that do not, pay a price. The cost is that the wound is always there. No escaping the knowledge that a normal adulthood will not be achieved. The sadness on me is like a drag on a swimmer and there are always unanswered questions. Did I do something wrong? Am I doing something wrong now? Parents of autistic children need all the help they can get.

My final session with Dora took place in late July 1979. She and I had developed a deep and lasting friendship that I would recall often in the next decades.

Chapter 15

Jean, Where Are You Now?

THIRTY-SEVEN YEARS AFTER my final interview with Dora, having just left my job of almost thirty years, it was time to keep my promise to her and find Jean.

I wondered whether she was thriving somewhere. Was she well cared for? Would she remember me? Would Dora, who had died in 1990, be pleased with the care Jean was receiving today?

Thinking that Jean might still be living in the East Bay, I began my search by calling the Chamber of Commerce and was directed to the East Bay Regional Center. I was delighted to find that Jean was in their system and had a caseworker who was responsive and eager to help. She had visited Jean routinely for the past fifteen years and assured me Jean was enjoying good health and lived in a comfortable home with four other women and a caretaker. No one but the caseworker had visited her in the twenty-plus years since her mother died. She gave me Jean's address and phone number.

I was thrilled to have found Jean and relieved to know she was doing well. I was eager to see her to let her know that after this long time she had not been forgotten.

As I was getting ready to call her, I sat back and began to recall the details of one of our last outings that was somehow typical of Jean, Dora, and myself. Though it occurred many years back, it was an indelible memory.

It had been a summer morning in July during my first year as Jean's companion. As prearranged, I was to spend the day with her. Knocking on the brown, wooden door of the family home, I noticed a Christmas tree ornament that Jean had made several years before, as well as a veiny mass of wires protruding from the hole where the doorbell was missing. All this had felt familiar and comfortable as I waited in the quiet air for the door to open.

I heard the stir of voices and feet within, and Jean opened the door. "Good morning, Phyllis Grilikhes," she'd said in a well-articulated, stilted voice, as though someone had drilled her in elocution lessons. I stood and waited while Dora and Jean bustled about in gentle, mother-daughter interaction. "Do you want your jacket? Here, take this one. That one doesn't go with what you're wearing. Where's your purse? Do you have your sunglasses?"

Dora's questioning had caused a flurry of whining and irritation in Jean, who could not find her sunglasses. When they were finally found, Jean and I left the house. That is, after her exit ritual, which meant running back to the door several times to touch her feet to the threshold. Meanwhile I got in the car and called to her that I was leaving—would she please come?

"Just joking," she said. "Not leaving, not really?"

This was followed by a high-pitched whine as she grimaced and pounded the side of her head with her fist. Swinging open the car door, she got in, then out, then in again several times, opened and closed the door, touched the ground, and so forth. Both of us in the car at last, Jean found my hand and, smiling, pressed it between her two dry and gentle ones. I responded by placing my hand on hers, telling her that I was happy to be with her. This scene had so explicitly expressed her affection at the time that I was astounded. I felt full of warmth and love for her.

The car finally in motion, Dora smiled from the window of the house and looked relieved as we drove off.

Back in the present moment, I dialed the

number the caseworker had given me. A pleasant voice answered the phone. In response I said, "Is Jean there? May I speak to her? I'm an old friend."

I waited, remembering her sly smile, how she would cover her mouth and whistle through her teeth when she was happy.

The phone was handed to her and I said, "Hello, Jean! This is Phyllis, your friend from long ago. Do you remember me?"

"Yes, I do. Phyllis Grilikhes!"

Relieved and encouraged, I asked if I could visit her.

"Come tomorrow? Work with me every day?"

As clear as if it was yesterday, I recalled those long-ago days. "No, but I'd like to see you." I offered a date, on a Monday, and she promised to mark the calendar.

When Jean opened the front door of her house on that Monday, we both stared in instant, quiet recognition. I'm not sure what she saw, but before me was the same intensely fragile, beautiful face, roughened by time. Her hair, once dark and in a long bob, was quite gray and cut very short. I felt a familiar tenderness and wanted to hug her, but held back. It occurred to me suddenly that through knowing Jean I had somehow gained a deeper knowing of myself. Even with the deep gulf that divided us, we shared similarities that I had felt from the beginning.

Jean looked well-cared for and was wearing a bright pink outfit. Smiling, a whimsical presence, she was still slender and restless. Her intelligence was, as it always had been, outwardly masked, yet I could tell she was keenly aware of what was going on around her.

I felt deeply glad and amazed to see her after all these years. In what seemed to be a clean and safe neighborhood, Carla, the care provider, was responsible for the well-being of Jean and four other highly-functioning women who shared the house. Jean showed me the bedroom she shared with her roommate.

Both women had adequate cubbies for their private belongings; the room was immaculate and tastefully decorated. Carla was an efficient house manager and took pride in keeping clean, orderly surroundings. Each person was responsible for daily chores and Jean liked to make the coffee. This had been her home for fifteen years.

Compared to years ago, Jean's behavior was surface-calm and subdued, possibly due to medication combined with a mellowness that tends to evolve with age.

We headed to lunch at a fast food joint that she loved. After a hamburger, she tested me. "I won't have coffee. May I have coffee?" She knew it was not good for her. I suggested tea (remembering her desire for chocolate donuts long ago when her mother had bought her sugar donuts instead, and not wanting to repeat that scene).

Not too disgruntled, and having decided herself not to have coffee, she ordered tea and poured in many packets of sugar. We took a walk in the nearby park. I felt close to her, like a long-ago sister. She let me take her arm as we walked, or sort of tramped along in her usual way. The old arm-in-arm felt so good.

After our visit I dropped her off at a place she called "the Program." Vans used for transporting disabled adults were parked outside a large warehouse. Inside was a vast room where games, painting, socializing, and other activities were available. The atmosphere felt warm and accepting.

I asked Jean what she liked to do there. "Puzzles sometimes," she said. Unfortunately, nothing seemed to hold her interest for long. She did like to curl up on the couch, and perhaps enjoyed just being part of a place that provided a humane and steady sense of welcome.

I went back to visit her at "the Program" every few months over the following year, and each time she opened up to me more, perhaps because she knew I would return again soon.

A wonderful example of Jean allowing me into her life a bit more occurred at the end of one of those visits. She asked to go into the building and get her Log, a folder kept for each person attending the Program. Bringing it out to the car, she asked if I had paper and pen, and we wrote short notes back and forth. Then she took one of the notes I'd written, tucked it into an envelope in her Log, and ran to put the Log back into place with the others.

At one point I asked where she went every day. "To school," she said. Dora would have been pleased to hear that; even though the Program is a day care center and not a school.

On my third visit, she was lying on the couch against the back wall in the building when I told her it was time for me to leave. Lifting up suddenly, she planted a light kiss on my lips, then immediately laid down on the couch with her hands covering her face. Profoundly moved, I could hardly believe what she had done.

Flooded with warm feelings, I gently placed my hand on hers and said that I had really enjoyed seeing her again, and that I remembered the good times we had shared years ago. We both knew I couldn't visit her every day as in the past, so there was no way we could relive those times.

Saying goodbye, I left her on the couch and promised we would plan another visit soon and she could mark the calendar.

Opening the door into the blazing sun of the parking lot, I walked to my car and drove away feeling a sad pull, having to leave her there.

No blame here but a tale told
Of the devastation of lives
Within the nexus of a family
Each need subverted
By the tremendous need of another
With no answers that could compensate
For the price each one had paid

Final Thoughts

HOW DIFFERENT THE LIVES of Jean's parents and her treatment would have been had she been born today, or even forty years later than she was.

In 2012, researchers using brain imaging techniques were able to identify marked differences in the white cell matter (fibers that surround neurons and support transmission of neural signals) among six-month-old babies who would later develop Autism Spectrum Disorder. These changes in the brain cells were visible six months to a year before the affected children typically showed the full range of outward signs of autism.

Did Jean have this anomaly? No one knew. Her childhood was a design in futility. It is likely she was born with an innate defect and suffered the imprinting of severe stress in infancy and childhood. Quite possibly those indelible markings contributed to an overlay of secondary behavioral problems, which worsened over time.

As a child she had none of the benefits of treatment that exist today. Would early diagnosis and intervention have made a small difference, a huge difference, or no difference in her life, her condition too severe?

Had a realistic appraisal of her limitations been available, her parents might have been spared the heartache of false hope and wild optimism based on Jean's "bits of progress." She might have had a less frustrating course at Langley Porter had her condition been accepted as irreversible. But would her parents have been more willing to institutionalize her?

I sense that even if Jean had been one of Leo Kanner's early cases, Dora would still have made strong efforts on Jean's behalf to make certain that institutionalization would not be the final stopping place for her daughter.

Appendix:
Current Research
Findings on Diagnosis

From the Center for Autism and the Developing Brain at the Weill Cornell Medical College, New York-Presbyterian Hospital, Catherine Lord, Ph. D., Director reports in her article in the Journal of Consulting and Clinical Psychology, (Lord et al. 2012):

> *In young children—especially under two and a half years—we shouldn't treat autism as a lifetime diagnosis. We can offer parents some hope that a very young child might move out of the autism spectrum at the same time, others will regress whether or not they receive treatment and the reasons are unknown. A preliminary diagnosis is not for a lifetime."*

Autism Intervention Research Program director and professor at the University of California, San Diego, Laura Schreibman, strongly advises parents of the following:

> *A "wait and see" approach is not appropriate when autism is suspected. She says further that "delaying a*

diagnosis can mean giving up the signifi-cant gains of intervention that have been demonstrated before age six. It is impor-tantly noted by clinicians who work with very young children that it is the earli-ness of the intervention—not the method itself—that leads to positive outcomes, stressing further that there is more than one way to get a good outcome.

Although researchers have not been able to pinpoint the exact causes of autism, they are getting closer and know that this condition results from a genetic mutation in fifteen to twenty percent of cases and that environmental factors can combine with and increase genetic susceptibility.

In "Genes, Circuits, and Precision Therapies for Autism and Related Neurodevelopmental Disorders" by researchers Mustafa Sahin and Mriganka Sur in *Science* 20 Nov 2015: Vol. 350, Issue 6263, pp 923-924:

Research in the genetics of neurode-velopmental disorders, such as autism, suggests that several hundred genes are likely involved as risk factors for these disorders. This heterogeneity presents both a challenge and an opportunity for researchers. Although the exact identity of many of the genes remains to be discovered, functional analysis of genes underlying several single-gene disorders has yielded considerable progress.

Related Readings

In a Different Key: The Story of Autism
by John Donvan and Caren Zucker (2016)

NeuroTribes: The Legacy of Autism and the Future of Neurodiversity
by Steve Silberman (2015)

An Anthropologist on Mars
by Oliver Sacks (1995)

The Man Who Mistook His Wife for a Hat
by Oliver Sacks (1985)

The Siege
by Clara Claiborne Park (1968)

Childhood and Society
by Erik H. Erikson (1950 first edition; 1963 second edition)

Notes

1. "Case Report: Follow-up Study of Erik Erikson's Jean in His Book *Childhood and Society* (1963, second edition)."

2. Langley Porter Neuropsychiatric Institute, founded in 1943, was the first psychiatric hospital and clinic in California. It was cooperatively conceived and was named after Robert Langley Porter, Dean of the Medical School at the University of California, San Francisco, who had done much of the planning.

3. Erik Homberger Erikson (1902-1994) was an original thinker and world-famous psychoanalyst with broad interests. He published eight books; his first and best-known work is the classic *Childhood and Society* (1963). He received a Pulitzer Prize and National Book Award for *Gandhi's Truth* (1969).

   Professor Erikson contributed a profound theory on the eight stages of life. In his theory he emphasized the role of culture and society in human development. He addressed the many problems that can arise at every period of life from infancy onward. Each stage brings a particular psychological struggle that contributes to an important aspect of personality and psychosocial exchange. For example, the need for trust in infancy asks the existential question, Can I trust the world? Jean's infancy, for example, for whatever reasons did not seem to engender trust. In staircase fashion the stages proceed from childhood and adolescence, to young adulthood, middle adulthood, and older adulthood. One very important aspect of Erikson's theory is that he believed a person to be adaptable to growth and positive change throughout the life cycle.

Erikson was born in Germany to Danish parents. He came to the United States in 1933 and became Boston's first child analyst. He obtained a position at Harvard and later held positions at Yale, University of California, Berkeley, and the Menninger Foundation. Erikson returned to California to the Center for Advanced Study in the Behavioral Sciences at Palo Alto and later to the Mount Zion Hospital in San Francisco, where he was a clinician and psychiatric consultant.

4. John Watson (1878-1958) was a well-known behavioral psychologist and one of the fathers of behaviorism. His book *Psychological Care of Infant and Child* (1928) was published and widely read in the late twenties and early thirties.

5. A child's idiosyncratic response to sounds is explained by E. M. Ornitz in "The modulation of sensory input and motor output in autistic children," *Journal of Autism and Childhood Schizophrenia 4* (1974): 197-215.

6. Jean Piaget (1896-1980) was a Swiss developmental psychologist and philosopher, and the first psychologist to make a systematic study of cognitive development. His theory focuses on how children interact with their environment to develop complex reasoning and knowledge. His contributions include detailed observational studies and a series of simple but ingenious tests to reveal different ways that children think at different developmental stages. Piaget's theory assumes an intact nervous system. Due to unknown factors, autistic language development follows an idiosyncratic course.

7. Donald Winnicott (1896-1971), an English pediatrician and psychoanalyst, used the term

"transitional objects" to mean an object of affection that the child uses as substitute for a mother. *Winnicott Life and Work,* F. Robert Rodman, M.D. (2003): 164-166, 174.

8. John Bowlby (1907-1990) was a British psychologist, psychiatrist, and psychoanalyst known for his interest in child development and especially for his pioneering work on attachment in *A Secure Base: Parent-Child Attachment and Healthy Human Development* (1988). Attachment theory in infants "is primarily a process of *proximity seeking* to an identified *attachment figure* in situations of perceived distress or alarm for the purpose of survival. Infants become attached to adults who are sensitive and responsive in social interactions with the infant." *The Origins of Attachment Theory: John Bowlby and Mary Ainsworth,* Inge Bretherton (1992).

9. The Menninger Clinic established the Southard School for children in 1926. The school fostered treatment programs for children and adolescents and was recognized worldwide.

10. Bruno Bettelheim (1903-1990) founded the Orthogenic School in 1915 at the University of Chicago as a residential treatment center for autistic children. He was a prominent proponent of the theory that autistic behaviors stem from emotional frigidity of the child's mother. He authored many articles and books, two of the most famous being *Love Is Not Enough: The Treatment of Emotionally Disturbed Children* (1950) and *The Empty Fortress: Infantile Autism and the Birth of the Self* (1967).

11. Emma Pendleton Bradley Home provides residential treatment and school services for children with mental and neurological impairments.

12. Stanislaus Szurek (1907-1992) was a psychoanalyst and Director of Children's Services at Langley Porter Neuropsychiatric Institute and author of *Clinical Studies in Childhood Psychoses* (1973). His research interests were broad and he was always eager to explore partially solved diagnostic and therapeutic problems. He was especially interested in psychotic manifestations in children.

13. Leo Kanner (1894-1981) of Johns Hopkins University was the first physician in the United States to be identified as a child psychiatrist. His textbook, *Child Psychiatry* (1935), first described the syndrome of infantile autism. The syndrome was not well known until he authored a paper entitled "Autistic Disturbance of Affective Contact" (1943). His concise and cogent clinical descriptions of children with autism continue to inform, and are the standard against which current diagnostic criteria are measured. He was the first scientist to clearly define autism. His description of symptoms are known as Kanner's Syndrome.

    It should be noted that at the same time of Leo Kanner's findings, Hans Asperger was developing his own theory independently. It seemed at the time very similar to Kanner's clinical discovery of autism. Asperger's Syndrome, however, includes more basic abilities in the areas of language, social contact, and communication.

14. The Berkeley Activity Center is now known as the East Bay Activity Center. It was organized and developed in the spring of 1952 by Jean's mother, and other interested individuals, including a professor of clinical psychology at the University of California, Berkeley, and a clinical psychologist with the Berkeley public school system. At the time they expressed the purpose of the fledgling organization in the following words: "to offer a limited group of emotionally disturbed or mentally ill children the same educational and recreational

opportunities which contribute to the physical well-being and social growth of *all* children."

Implicit in the philosophy was the thought that, while progress might take place, criteria for acceptance into the program would not be based on the likelihood of success. The center was conceived as a pilot project, to pioneer in action research with children who were more emotionally disturbed than neurotic. An additional goal was to offer a training facility for teachers and counselors in the field.

Lorna Wing, British psychiatrist and mother of an autistic daughter, said, "I do believe you need autistic traits for real success in science and the arts, and I am fascinated by the behaviors and personalities of musicians and scientists. One of my favorite sayings is that nature never draws a line without smudging it. You cannot separate into those "with and those without" traits as they are so scattered." (*Psychology Today,* August 2014.)

15. Napa State Hospital is a psychiatric hospital in Napa, California, founded in 1875. One of California's five state hospitals, Napa State houses civil and forensic patients. It was once known for being a harsh environment.

16. Bernard Rimland (1928-2006) was an American research psychologist who founded the Autism Society of America in 1965 and the Autism Research Institute in 1967. He was a writer, lecturer, and advocate for children with developmental disorders. He wrote *Infantile Autism: The Syndrome and Its Implications for a Neural Theory of Behavior* (1964).

He is credited by many with changing the prevailing view of autism, in the field of psychiatry, from an emotional illness—widely thought to be caused by refrigerator mothers—to the current recognition that autism is a neurodevelopmental disorder. Rimland lectured on autism and related problems throughout the world, including before thousands of professional groups. He was the author of numerous publications.

In 1988 he served as the primary technical advisor on autism for the movie *Rain Man*. The movie helped establish worldwide awareness of this condition, just when its prevalence was becoming apparent.

17. Ivar Lovaas (1927-2010) was a Norwegian American clinical psychologist. The decades of contributions he made to the field of applied research led him to be known as the father of applied behavioral analysis (ABA). He developed a specialized technique applying behavior modification to autistic people.

The Lovaas Method used positive and negative reinforcement strategies to eliminate unwanted behaviors and encourage desirable behaviors. In his original studies in the late 1950's, aversive stimuli such as electric shock was used. He successfully treated many individuals engaging in extreme self-injury (eye gouging, head banging) where life expectancy was reduced by secondary infection.

The Lovaas Method includes high treatment intensity up to 40 hours per week in a 1:1 teaching setting using discrete trials; treatment is done at home with parents involved in every aspect of treatment. The curriculum is highly individualized with a heavy emphasis on teaching language. He contributed in major ways to the Autism Society of America, published hundreds of research articles and books, received state and national awards, and had his evidence-based teaching programs adopted by school districts. His work influenced how autism was treated and improved the lives of children stricken with the autism diagnosis worldwide.

18. The Lanterman-Petris-Short Act was coauthored by California State Assemblyman Frank D. Lanterman and California State Senators Nicholas

C. Petris and Alan Short. It was signed into law in 1967 by Governor Ronald Reagan and went into full effect on July 1, 1972. Under the act, patients were released from mandatory commitments in mental hospitals due to the availability of psychotropic pharmaceutical drugs. It seemed possible for many patients to be released into the community to live in board and care homes. Dora worked to get the Lanterman-Petris-Short Act passed. Eventually, however, funds for mental health were cut and many of the board and care homes were closed, leaving many mental patients without a home.

19. Gateway House is known at present as Gateway Center of Monterey County, Inc. Gateway Center is a private, not-for-profit community-based organization which provides a wide range of services, including residential care, developmental training, and activity programs for adults ages eighteen and over with intellectual disabilities.

20. The Berkeley Creative Wellness Center is a unique client-centered adult mental health day program based upon the unique needs of the individuals who attend it.

Acknowledgements

Profound thanks to Phyllis Aboaf, Anne Blackman, Toni Illick, Miriam Kammen, Elaine Mannon, George Shardlow for their generosity of time, insightful suggestions and unwavering friendship.

Deep appreciation to Ross Maxwell, my husband, whose understanding and encouragement from the start championed this book to its completion.

A debt of gratitude to Arianna Kenyon, my computer assistant, whose patience and generosity of spirit were deeply appreciated.

Thank you to my excellent editor, Darlene Frank, whose intelligence, good sense and expertise were indispensable.

It is a pleasure to thank Mark Weiman of Regent Press for his creative approach in the excellent handling of my book.

A note of thanks also to Cristina Deptula, publicist, for her efforts to promote my work.

About the Author

Phyllis Grilikhes, PhD, is publishing her second book, *Autism's Stepchild, A Mother's Story.* Her first book, a poetic narrative, *To Set A Light In Every Tunnel: The Story of a Life* was published by Regent Press in 2008.

A former dancer, currently retired from college teaching, she is an author, a licensed psychologist, a classical pianist and tapestry maker . . . who believes that we are all more than one thing.

CPSIA information can be obtained
at www.ICGtesting.com
Printed in the USA
FSOW03n0806131116